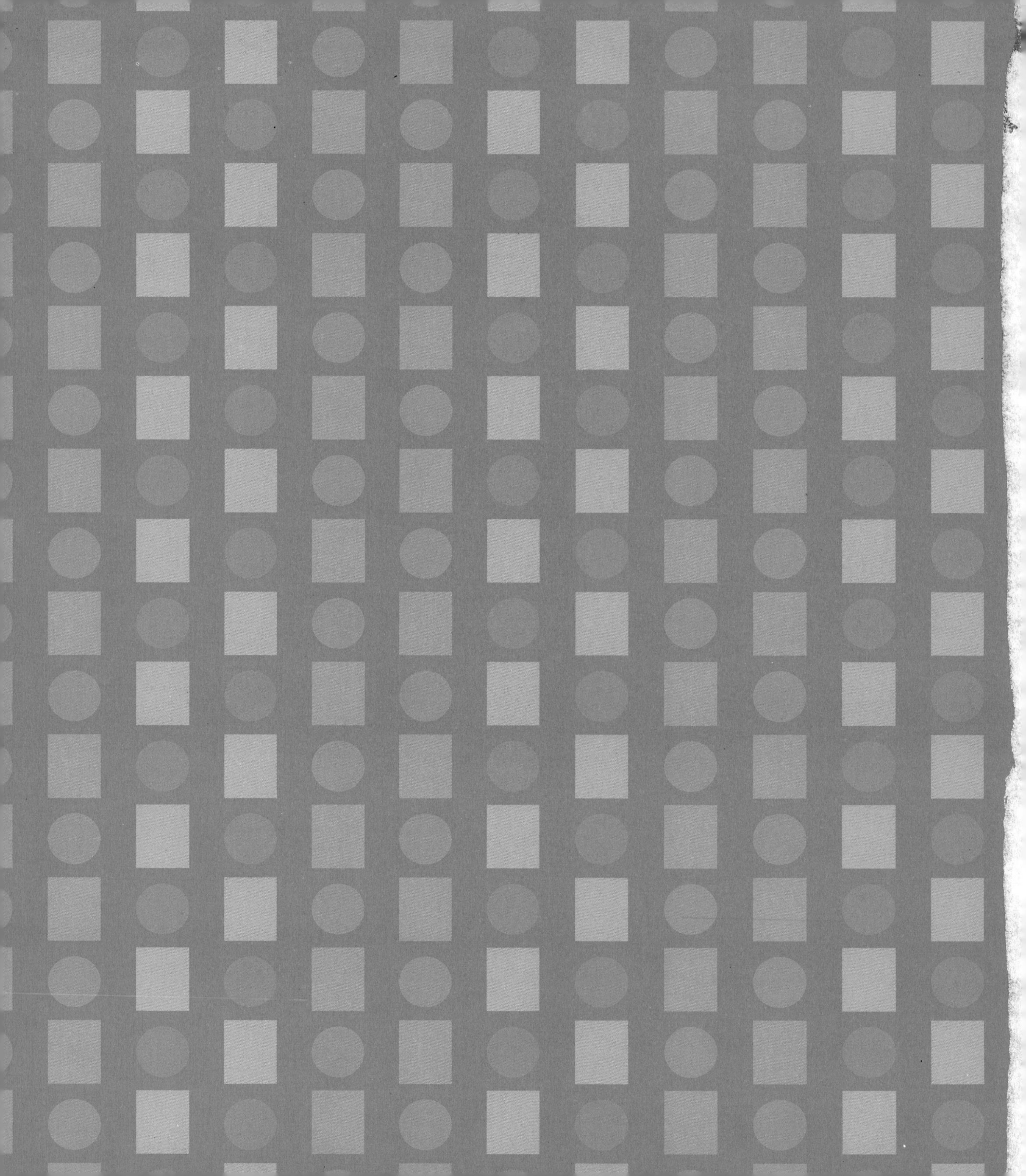

matthew kenney's mediterranean cooking

great flavors for the american kitchen

by matthew kenney and sam gugino

photographs by paul franz-moore

CHRONICLE BOOKS
SAN FRANCISCO

acknowledgments

Kirsten Kenney

Sandrine Lago • Matthew Scully

Karen Miele • Ricardo Amaral • Gennaro Picone

Karine Bakhoum • David Pearlberg • Sig Bergamin • Jane Dystel

Mel Tortorici • Kelly Kochendorfer • Cathy Young

The entire staff at Matthew's • The entire staff at Mezze

Bill LeBlond • Susan Derecskey

Library of Congress Cataloging-in-Publication Data:
Kenney, Matthew.
Matthew Kenney's Mediterranean cooking: great flavors for the American kitchen/by Matthew Kenney and Sam Gugino; photographs by Paul Franz-Moore.
p. cm.
Includes index.
ISBN 0-8118-1443-2 (hc)
1. Cookery, Mediterranean I. Gugino, Sam. II. Title
TX725.M35K46 1997
641.59'1822—dc21 97-12218
CIP

Printed in Hong Kong.

Book and cover design by Jill Jacobson

Distributed in Canada by Raincoast Books
8680 Cambie Street
Vancouver, British Columbia V6P 6M9

10 9 8 7 6 5 4 3 2 1

Chronicle Books
85 Second Street
San Francisco, California 94105

Web Site: www.chronbooks.com

Shown on front cover: Sautéed Sea Scallops with Spicy Orange Dressing, page 21.

dedication

To Robert, Shirley, Maryellen, and Patrick Kenney

—M.K.

To Mary Lee Keane

—S.G.

Matthew's

table of contents

introduction

At first, my curiosity was piqued by the dramatic blue, black, and rust-orange awning, the warm red tiles out front, and the compelling etched logo. But what really hooked me as I passed by Malvasia, a restaurant that was about to open on the Upper East Side of New York, was the menu.

Was it Greek? Moroccan? Egyptian? The dishes certainly sounded Italian, but the duck with dried figs and Sicilian olives, for example, did not register as Italian food in my mind. Nor did the lobster salad with avocado and hearts of palm. Or the charcoal-grilled octopus with caperberries and spicy olive oil.

Day after day during my lunch break from the press office of Christie's Auction House where I worked, I went to Malvasia as if drawn by some irresistible force. I watched as the restaurant slowly took shape. With each new visit a bit more of Malvasia's personality emerged. Then one day the restaurant manager, who had been noticing me, came out and asked if I wanted a job as a waiter. "But I don't have any experience," I protested. "No problem," he assured me.

Malvasia's mysterious and exhilarating food and its inviting design had such a strong impact on me that I was ready to change careers right then and there. And I did. It didn't take long for me to realize, though, that the real creativity in a restaurant lies more in preparing food than in serving it. Two months later I was in the kitchen, learning chef Gennaro Picone's secrets of getting the most out of foods by infusing them with bold flavors.

Afterward, at the French Culinary Institute and at the classic French restaurant, La Caravelle, I refined my techniques and continued to grow as a chef. But I never lost the essence of what I learned at Malvasia. In fact, during the creation of Matthew's, my own restaurant, I retained the basic concepts of Malvasia, adding to them as I learned more about Mediterranean cooking.

Since then I've created a second restaurant, Mezze, and by the time this book is published a third, Monzù, will be open. All are quite different and in total they span the breadth of the Mediterranean as this book does. Maybe I should rename my restaurant corporation, Mediterranean Rim, Inc.

Matthew's

Matthew's seems as if it could be in Casablanca or Tangiers, a reflection of my love of Moroccan cuisine. Look into the expansive windows from bustling Third Avenue on Manhattan's Upper East Side and you'll see a cool, soothing place where leafy ferns and palms seem to sway as overhead fans gently whir. Beyond the entrance, paved with Spanish floor tiles and shrouded in muslin curtains, there are wide-planked oak floors, rattan chairs, crisp, white table tops, and a copper-topped bar with forties beaded lamp fixtures. Sometimes I expect Sidney Greenstreet to stroll in off the street for lunch.

Mezze, located in midtown Manhattan, gives the feel of a sunny outdoor Greek taverna on a secluded Athens side street. High, white-washed walls are dotted with blue window shutters and French doors that look as if someone is about to open them at any moment. Follow the earth-toned tiles from the espresso bar in front to the juice bar in back and you'll come upon our open kitchen where we lay out flatbread sandwiches on a zinc-topped bar every afternoon. Across the way is a salad bar filled with elements of an eastern Mediterranean Rim mezze like twice-cooked eggplant salad and spiced carrots. While the food at Matthew's is very approachable, Mezze brings my concept of Mediterranean food down to an even more elemental level. For example, it could be as simple as making a Mediterranean BLT with Middle Eastern flatbread instead of American white bread, prosciutto instead of bacon, and arugula instead of iceberg lettuce.

Monzù is named after the Sicilian chefs who cooked a sophisticated cuisine based on many principles of French haute cuisine. And the restaurant will reflect that high level of cooking and dining. It will have the same breezy feel as Matthew's but with a totally different decor featuring all the colors of the sun, from lemon yellow to burnt orange to pomegranate red.

My travels in the lands around the Mediterranean brought many culinary revelations. One was eating grilled pigeon in Egypt. The sensual satisfaction of tearing apart the warm, crisp bird with my fingers, then dipping it into cool, soothing tahini-yogurt sauce was incredible. Another was a plate of fettuccine topped with shaved, fresh white truffles in Milan during the peak of truffle season. The truffles, kept under glass domes like jewels in almost every restaurant, were intoxicating. The simplicity and freshness of these dishes was markedly different from the more distant and formal French cooking I'd done at La Caravelle and the French Culinary Institute. I also discovered the spices and slow cooking techniques of North Africa, and the powerful cheeses of Spain. Olives and capers became my secret weapons.

After a few years of tasting Mediterranean Rim foods in their native lands, translating it at home and in restaurants, and thinking about it almost constantly, I finally figured out what my cooking was all about: Mediterranean Rim cuisine done in America. Thus were sown the first seeds of this book. I also learned that I could share this approach with home cooks. And so I set out to adapt classic combinations and preparations to suit average Americans.

The term "Mediterranean cuisine" is certainly not new to us. But "Mediterranean Rim" cuisine probably is. Why the difference in terminology? All too often when reference is made to the Mediterranean, the focus is primarily on Spain, France, Italy, and perhaps Greece. But the concept of the Mediterranean Rim is more encompassing and includes, for example, Morocco and the other countries of North Africa, as well as those of the eastern Mediterranean, from Egypt to Turkey. This broadens the concept of the cuisine of the region considerably. In some ways it is akin to the difference between using the term Asian cuisine, which pretty much limits the concept to the Asian mainland (except perhaps for Japan), and Pacific Rim cuisine, which incorporates Australia, New Zealand, Indonesia, and the other islands of the Pacific.

The spices and cooking techniques of Morocco alone—a country which many don't even consider in the Mediterranean because of its perch on the far western end of the Mediterranean Rim—add enormous complexity to the concept of Mediterranean cooking. Morocco and the other often overlooked countries of the Mediterranean Rim not only bring their indigenous cooking to Mediterranean Rim cuisine, they also bring the influences of countries outside the region, countries like Persia and India, even such distant countries as Japan. Thus, you'll see in my cooking curry, yogurt, cumin, tahini, and panko (Japanese bread crumbs) in addition to basil, garlic, and olive oil.

We have been hearing for some time how the so-called Mediterranean Diet is one of the most healthful on the planet, with reliance on heart-healthy olive oil instead of butter as well as on vegetables, fruits, and grains. We have also seen an explosion of Mediterranean-style restaurants as well as numerous Mediterranean Rim dishes in other restaurants.

While we are seeing more and more Mediterranean and Mediterranean-style products on the market—from a slew of balsamic vinegars to vegetables like purslane—I've seen few distillations of Mediterranean Rim cooking with ingredients readily available to most Americans. So I've tried to stay away from using exotic ingredients in this book as much as possible. No truffle oil or orange flower water. And the few times I use somewhat unusual ingredients, I give alternatives or mail order sources. I've also eliminated the need for special equipment. No couscoussière is needed for the couscous or tagine for the Moroccan stew of the same name.

Nor do you need special skills to make the recipes in this book work properly. Most of the methods are simple and straightforward. And even those that are a little on the long side don't require expertise, just a bit of patience.

A good example of this is the Red Lettuces with Spiced Almonds, Green Olives, and Manchego Cheese inspired by a cheese plate I had some years ago at Mad 61 restaurant in New York. This became the signature salad of Matthew's. The red lettuces, spiced almonds, olives, and manchego cheese offer an unusual array of textures and flavors in a well-rounded and stunningly simple dish.

Another significant aspect to my cooking is the use of homemade condiments, sauces, and dressings, such as Mint Chutney and Tomato Jam. These simply prepared but intensely flavored elements can be used with many dishes. This allows home cooks to take basic dishes like roasts and make them more interesting.

Because quality ingredients are the hallmark of Mediterranean Rim cooking, the Pantry chapter is an especially important part of this book. In the past dozen years or so there has been a huge influx of outstanding raw materials, not only in ethnic enclaves of major cities but in mainstream supermarkets across the country. In addition to imported ingredients, we are seeing more and more first-rate foodstuffs produced in the United States, such as olive oils from California and wild mushrooms from the Pacific Northwest. I like bold and intense flavors and so I use ingredients that carry these flavors like dried fruits, nuts, olives, honey, and lemons. These ingredients also minimize elaborate techniques and long cooking times.

Ultimately, what I've tried to accomplish in this book is to bring the flavors of the Mediterranean Rim to you as simply and as easily as possible while still maintaining their authenticity. For example, I've found that the flavor of chicken with olives and preserved lemons—a classic Mediterranean Rim dish if ever there was one—can be achieved with lemon zest and fresh lemon juice instead of waiting a week for the lemons to be preserved. This dish may not be made authentically, but it certainly tastes authentic. And what is more important? Besides, who has the time, space, or inclination to preserve lemons?

But even authentic food—whether it's prepared or tastes that way—doesn't always meet the requirements of the American consumer for appearance. The fact that they eat it that way in Andalusia or Apulia is beside the point. So I've taken liberties with my versions of classic Mediterranean Rim dishes to make them look great as well as taste great.

A good example is the two ways I've modified the Moroccan lamb tagine, a stew with cubes of meat. In one instance, Braised Lamb Shank with Dried Apricots, I use a more impressive-looking whole lamb shank, but the dish retains the same rich flavors of a classic tagine. When I do use cubes of meat, as in Lamb Tagine with Dried Figs and Almonds, I finish the dish with a crisp nut crust. Tagines are also often too sweet for Americans, so I toned down the sweetness in both while keeping the character of the original.

I hope this book will excite you the way my journey through the cuisines of the Mediterranean Rim has excited me. Don't keep it on the shelf just for weekends. I want you to use it as often as you can. Think of it not as a bible but as a map to help you on your own culinary explorations.

pantry

A well-stocked pantry need not contain truffles and a dozen types of olive oil. Rather, it should hold basic but intensely flavored ingredients, which allow you to put together a variety of dishes in a short amount of time and with minimal effort. Thus armed, you can turn a plain piece of chicken into a delight with olives, almonds, and saffron. The juice from a can of Italian plum tomatoes enables you to transform rice into a delicious tomato risotto. And canned chick peas may quickly become hummus, the basis of a soup, or an easy bean salad. As you can see from the list below, it is a simple matter to span the Mediterranean Rim with a reasonably well-stocked pantry.

Building a pantry requires some thought, much like building a wine cellar. Begin by writing down some of your favorite nonperishable ingredients; olives, dried fruits, and nuts, for example, are always part of my pantry. Use the following list of ingredients as a blueprint for your own pantry, adding or subtracting to suit your personal needs and tastes.

ANCHOVIES Fillets are the most common, flat in 2-ounce cans, upright in jars or wrapped around capers. I prefer whole anchovies packed in salt because they are meatier. They're available in specialty food shops or by mail order (see page 161).

BEANS (CANNED) Chick peas are among the best canned beans. Others vary in quality (cannellini beans are often mushy, for example), so find a brand you can rely on. It may not be the same for each kind of bean.

BREAD CRUMBS I make my own fresh bread crumbs from day-old Italian or French bread. Some markets and bakeries sell fresh bread crumbs.
Panko: Japanese bread crumbs with a light texture, available at Japanese and Asian markets or by mail order (see page 161)

CAPERS Generally available in two sizes pickled in a vinegar brine. The smaller ones dole out their pungency in smaller bursts. Specialty food stores carry large capers packed in salt.

CHEESE *Parmesan:* The most versatile and important cheese in Mediterranean cooking. Use the real thing, Parmigiano-Reggiano. It's worth the extra cost.
OTHERS: *Pecorino, fresh mozzarella, manchego, cabrales, feta,* and *goat cheeses.* Since cheeses don't last indefinitely, it's not advisable to keep all on hand. Buy one or two at a time, rotating periodically.

FRUITS, DRIED Ubiquitous throughout the Mediterranean Rim. I most frequently use apricots, figs, dates, and raisins (golden and black). These days almost any fruit comes in dried form, so try, for example, dried cherries or cranberries.

GRAINS *Couscous:* Actually a kind of pasta, though used like a grain. It is almost always found in instant form but the quality is often good.

Bulgur: Steamed, dried, and crushed wheat kernels (not cracked wheat). Now commonly available in cereal-size boxes in supermarkets. When sold loose in ethnic markets and health food stores it often comes in two or three different grinds.

Barley: An ancient grain used mostly for bread, beer, and soup. It can be an excellent substitute for rice in grain salads and risottos. Widely available in supermarkets.

Rice: See page 14.

HERBS Most major supermarkets now carry at least several fresh herbs. I use mint, basil, and cilantro most often. They offer more subtle seasoning than rosemary, sage, thyme, chives, and marjoram. For parsley, I prefer the more flavorful flat-leaf or Italian parsley to the curly type. Fresh herbs will last up to a week, loosely bagged in plastic in the crisper section of your refrigerator. The only dried herb I use is bay leaves.

HONEY I frequently use honey to balance the harshness of spices and acids or to brush on meats to help them caramelize during roasting. Plain supermarket honey is fine, but it's worth seeking out flavored ones like wildflower, lavender, orange blossom, or thyme.

LEMONS I'd be lost without lemons because I use their juice and zest in just about everything. Though technically a perishable item, lemons are available year-round and they keep well, so there's no excuse for buying the bottled stuff.

MUSHROOMS, DRIED If fresh wild mushrooms are not available, dried mushrooms, particularly shiitake, porcini, and morels are usually good substitutes. Because they are intensely flavored, a small amount goes a long way.

MUSTARD A full-flavored, Dijon style is the most versatile.

NUTS Almonds are my favorite and I use them in several forms—whole, sliced, and chopped. I also use a lot of pine nuts, hazelnuts, and sesame seeds. Walnuts and pistachios are less common in my pantry but worth having on hand. Tightly sealed at room temperature, nuts stay fresh up to six weeks. They last longer when refrigerated (up to four months) or frozen (up to six months), both good ideas in summer. Toasting increases the flavor.

OILS *Olive oil:* The sine qua non ingredient of any Mediterranean Rim pantry. It is used in everything from sautéing to salads. I use the more flavorful extra virgin type in salads and marinades and for cooking vegetables. Pure olive oil is used for sautéing or frying. Every country in the Mediterranean Rim produces olive oil. I use Italian, the most common, but you should experiment with oils from Greece, Spain, France, or Morocco, just as you would with wines.

Nut oils: Also used extensively along the Mediterranean Rim and now more widely available in the United States. Almond, hazelnut, and walnut oils are all worth trying, but it's probably impractical to keep all three in your pantry. Well-sealed in a cool, dry place, they'll last about three months, considerably longer under refrigeration.

Other oils: When a neutral oil is called for in deep-frying recipes, for example, I prefer canola oil for its high smoke point and heart-healthy qualities. Lately, I've been using a blend of 70 percent canola and 30 percent olive oil that has become popular with chefs for cooking instead of pure olive oil or 100 percent canola. There are also many flavored oils on the market. I like the Consorzio line in particular. You can also make your own.

spicy olive oil

makes about 2 cups

2 cups pure olive oil

1 tablespoon crushed red pepper

Put the olive oil and red pepper in a medium saucepan over medium-low heat. Cook for 15 minutes, being careful not to simmer or boil. Remove from the heat and let cool at room temperature.

Strain the oil through a fine mesh strainer lined with cheesecloth into a glass jar. Cover and let stand at room temperature for 7 to 10 days before using.

OLIVES I like to have on hand at least two black varieties of olives and two green. One black variety is oil-cured—that is to say, not in brine—like those from Morocco or Sicily, and one in brine such as a meaty Greek kalamata, tiny French nicoise, or Italian gaeta. Green olives may be Spanish, French picholines, or jumbo Sicilians.

ONION FAMILY Though onions, garlic, shallots, and green onions are perishable, I consider them pantry staples because I use them so regularly.

Garlic: Whole heads are available year-round and will last several weeks without refrigeration if kept cool.

Green onions: Also known as scallions, they are available year-round. The tops can be substituted for chives as a garnish.

Onions: Any white or Spanish onion is fine in most recipes that call for cooked onions. When using the onions raw, I prefer sweet onions such as Vidalia, Walla Walla, or Maui, which have less of a bite.

Shallots: Also available year-round. When they cannot be found, onions mixed with garlic are a decent substitute. Green onions are not because they are too mild.

PASTA I use dried pasta in most of the dishes in my restaurants and the recipes in this book because I find the quality superior to fresh pasta. And, of course, the convenience is unbeatable. I use DeCecco brand but there are many other good pasta imports from Italy.

PASTES Prepared pesto, tapenade, and olive paste are handy to have for quick hors d'oeuvre spreads or sauces.

POMEGRANATE MOLASSES Pomegranate juice boiled to a thick, concentrated syrup. (There are also syrups of pomegranate that are thinner.) Available in Middle Eastern markets, specialty stores, and by mail order (see page 161). Also see Note, page 157.

RICE *Basmati:* A somewhat thin, long-grain, and fragrant Indian rice that cooks quicker than normal long grain rice. Also produced in the United States as Texmati. Available in white and brown versions.
Risotto rices: Arborio is the most commonly available; and it is fine for the recipes in this book. I use Vialone Nano because it holds up better under restaurant conditions. Carnaroli is another, less common variety.

ROASTED PEPPERS In jars, seeded and peeled, these are a valuable pantry item when convenience is essential or when fresh red bell peppers are prohibitively expensive.

SALT Not all salt is created equal. I prefer kosher salt because it is unadulterated and doesn't clump. Sea salt is excellent for marinating, curing, and smoking fish. I use table salt in pastry because it melts easily and maintains the dough's silky texture.

SPICES I favor whole spices which, like coffee in bean form, have more flavor than those already ground. Once ground, that pent-up flavor is released. So I recommend a spice mill (a coffee grinder used exclusively for spices) or mortar and pestle for smaller amounts. Cumin, cardamom, coriander, cayenne, and chilies are most often used in my kitchen. Though it is a mix of seasonings, a high-quality chili powder may be substituted for dried and ground chili peppers (most often the ancho variety). Other essential spices include crushed red pepper, black peppercorns (ground as needed), saffron (threads, not ground), curry powder, and ginger (fresh, candied, and ground). Also good to have on hand: cloves, allspice, whole nutmeg, cinnamon (ground and sticks), paprika, and fennel and anise seeds.

Matthew's

STOCK A well-made stock can make or break a soup and turn an ordinary braised dish into something special. The three stocks that follow can be made on a leisurely weekend and frozen for later use. Three suggestions:

- Always save shells, bones, and heads from seafood. You can freeze them until you get enough to make a stock.
- Buy poultry on the bone and bone the meat yourself, not only to save money but to have material for stock. Also save the giblets, except for the liver, and skin.
- Freeze the stock in practical portions such as one-pint containers. Even put some in ice trays for dishes that call for small amounts.

Canned stocks are OK in a pinch (though watch out for the salt), but a better choice might be the "homemade" stocks that are increasingly available in gourmet markets. Bottled clam juice is also quite salty, but I've found it useful in dishes like risotto.

chicken stock

makes 4 quarts

6 pounds chicken necks, backs, wings, and giblets (no livers)
2 medium onions, coarsely chopped
2 carrots, coarsely chopped
2 ribs celery, coarsely chopped
Green tops of 2 leeks, coarsely chopped
12 sprigs of parsley
2 sprigs of thyme
3 bay leaves
½ teaspoon black peppercorns

Thoroughly rinse the chicken parts under cold running water. Put in a large stockpot, cover with 6 quarts cold water, and bring to a boil over high heat. Skim the top of the stock to remove any foam as it forms.

Add the remaining ingredients, reduce to a simmer, and cook, uncovered, for 5 hours, skimming foam every 40 to 60 minutes.

Remove the chicken and vegetables with a wire mesh strainer or skimmer and strain the liquid through a cheesecloth-lined strainer into a 4-quart pot or heatproof plastic container. Put the container in ice in the sink or a large bowl until cooled to warm. Refrigerate. When completely cool, skim the fat that congeals on top. Bring to a boil before using. Refrigerate for up to 3 days. Freeze in small containers.

rich chicken stock

makes 2 quarts

2 pounds chicken, squab, pheasant, or duck necks, backs, wings, and giblets (no livers)
4 quarts Chicken Stock (page 15)
¼ cup dried mushrooms (optional)

Preheat the oven to 400 degrees. Thoroughly rinse the poultry parts under cold running water and pat dry. Place in a roasting pan and bake for 45 to 60 minutes, stirring every 20 minutes, or until medium brown.

Transfer the poultry parts to a large stockpot, add the stock and dried mushrooms, if using, and bring to a boil over high heat. Skim the top of the stock to remove any foam. Reduce to a simmer and cook for 2½ to 3 hours, skimming foam every 40 to 60 minutes.

Remove the solids with a wire mesh strainer or skimmer and strain the liquid through a cheesecloth-lined strainer into a 2-quart pot or heatproof plastic container. Put the container in ice in the sink or a large bowl until cooled to warm. Refrigerate. When completely cool, skim fat that congeals on top. Bring to a boil before using. Refrigerate for up to 3 days. Freeze in small containers.

shellfish stock

makes 2 quarts

2 pounds shrimp or lobster shells
¼ cup olive oil
2 cups dry white wine
1 cup fresh tomatoes or tomato scraps
2 medium onions, coarsely chopped
2 ribs celery, coarsely chopped
5 sprigs of parsley
3 sprigs of thyme
2 bay leaves
10 black peppercorns
Pinch of saffron (optional)

Rinse the shells under cold running water. Put the oil in a large stockpot over high heat. Add the shells and sauté for 12 to 14 minutes, stirring regularly. Add 4 quarts water and the remaining ingredients. Bring to a boil. Skim the top of the stock to remove any foam.

Reduce the heat and simmer for 1 hour and 20 minutes, skimming foam every 20 minutes. Remove the shells with a wire mesh strainer or skimmer and strain the liquid through a cheesecloth-lined strainer into a large (at least 4½ quarts) saucepan.

Bring to a boil and reduce the heat to a simmer. Reduce to 2 quarts, about 1 hour and 40 minutes. Cool in an ice bath in the sink or large bowl until warm. Refrigerate. When completely cool, skim the fat that congeals on top. Bring to a boil before using. Refrigerate for up to 3 days. Freeze in small containers.

TOMATOES *Canned:* When fresh tomatoes are out of season, canned Italian plum tomatoes in juice are an excellent alternative.

Oven-dried: To dry fresh tomatoes, preheat the oven to 200 degrees. Sprinkle the tomatoes with 2 tablespoons of the olive oil, and season with salt and pepper to taste. Place, cut side up, on a baking sheet and bake until partially dried but still retaining some moisture, about 1 hour and 40 minutes. Cut crosswise into ½-inch-wide slices and set aside.

Peeled and seeded: To peel fresh tomatoes, core them and put them in a pot with 2 quarts of boiling water for about 30 seconds. Remove, cool under running water, and peel. Halve, lengthwise, and gently squeeze to remove the seeds.

Sun-dried: Packed in oil, they are good for quick sauces, spreads, or dips.

TAHINI Sesame seed paste, available in better grocery stores and many supermarkets.

TUNA FISH Preferably Italian, packed in olive oil. Otherwise, use fancy albacore.

VINEGAR I use three vinegars in most of my cooking: red wine, sherry, balsamic. When something less acidic is called for, I use lemon juice rather than the milder white wine or rice vinegars.

WINES, LIQUEURS, AND SPIRITS Any wine you'd drink can be used in cooking. The same is true for port and liqueurs, particularly orange or other citrus and nut liqueurs like Frangelico or amaretto.

YOGURT Plain. Whole milk emulsifies better in sauces than low-fat versions.

appetizers, soups, and mezze

The cuisines of the Mediterranean Rim have helped to transform a sea of mundane American meal starters like shrimp cocktail and bland cream soups into dishes with the same bold and deep flavors we thought we could get only in entrees. Indeed, restaurant menus often have appetizers that are more interesting than the main courses. Thus, it has become commonplace for diners to order three appetizers as a meal, rather than an appetizer and an entree. This is the concept behind a common method of eating all along the Mediterranean Rim, whether it is the eastern Mediterranean mezze table, the Italian antipasto platter, or the Spanish tapas bar. Look at the recipes in this chapter and see what a delicious meal you can create from say, a platter of Cumin-Cured Salmon, Eggplant Puree with Yogurt and Mint, and some marinated Portuguese sardines (see pages 24–26).

Baked Squash Soup with Nuts and Spices

Mediterranean Rim soups are often quite hearty, more like stews. I prefer lighter, fresher soups that use seasonal produce. But while the soups in this chapter may not be exactly Mediterranean, they are, like so many other dishes in this book, reflective of the flavors of the Mediterranean Rim. The Chilled Chick Pea, Tomato, and Yogurt Soup, for example, captures the freshness of ripe, seasonal tomatoes and combines it with tangy yogurt and chick peas. The same is true for the Moroccan-inspired Baked Squash Soup with Nuts and Spices, though this soup would fit comfortably on an American Thanksgiving table since the hard-shell squash it uses comes from the New World.

Soups are appealing because they are simple and flexible. They can usually be prepared in one large pot and allow room for error because they are easily adjusted. If a soup is too thick, you can always add extra stock. If a little bland, just add a pinch of cayenne or chili powder.

When preparing a first course or a mezze table, keep in mind a few things. Whether eaten in the traditional American manner or as part of a mezze table, appetizers should provide a satisfying, distinctive taste that doesn't overwhelm the palate for an entree or other small dishes to come. This can be achieved with a variety of spice and herb combinations as well as changes in texture and the use of different cooking techniques such as marinating, curing, and grilling.

Colors should be attractive to excite the taste buds and heighten anticipation for the rest of the meal. Variety is also a major consideration. There should be pungent foods, as well as sweet, crisp, and soft foods. Variety doesn't mean cacophony, though. The dishes of a mezze table should always be in harmony.

No need to rely just on the recipes in this chapter either. There are candidates for your mezze, antipasto, or tapas meal in the Salad, Vegetable, and Seafood chapters like Sicilian-Style Rice Salad with Tuna and Mint, page 48; Artichokes Braised with Coriander, Lemon, and Garlic, page 118; Moroccan Spiced Carrots, page 123; and Spicy Shrimp Frittata, page 82.

Appetizers need not be complicated. You can fill a table with dishes that take no more than a few minutes each, such as cubes of feta cheese drizzled with olive oil and hot pepper; flatbread served with Za'atar, page 95, or tahini mixed with yogurt; chick peas right out of the can tossed with mint, olive oil, and lemon juice; and dates, plain or stuffed with almonds.

Although raw fennel is eaten at the end of the meal around the Mediterranean Rim, it can make the beginning of the meal a little more special. It's also a good substitute for celery or carrot sticks. Of course, good bread and breadsticks are always welcome. Flatbread, too, whether purchased or made from my recipe on page 159.

Don't be embarrassed to fill in with convenience items like roasted peppers in a jar (just toss them in olive oil and garlic); prepared tapenade or sun-dried tomatoes slathered on toasted bread; smoked and cured fish; and marinated olives. Even something as simple as paper-thin slices of prosciutto can be a luxurious appetizer.

While chilled white wine has become de rigueur at the beginning of many meals, it might be fun to drink what the Mediterraneans drink with their little dishes. In Spain, tapas are almost inseparable from sherry, particularly bone-dry fino sherry. In other parts of the Mediterranean Rim, anise-flavored drinks are drunk with appetizers. In France, it's pastis, in Greece, ouzo. Italians tend to favor bitter drinks like Campari and Punt e Mes. And if enthusiasm lags for any of these, there's always Champagne.

sautéed sea scallops with spicy orange dressing

serves 6

1 medium bulb fennel
7 tablespoons olive oil
3 tablespoons lemon juice
Salt and freshly ground black pepper
2 cups freshly squeezed orange juice
1 teaspoon ancho chili powder or chili powder mix
2 tablespoons unsalted butter
¼ cup all-purpose flour
1 ½ tablespoons ground cumin
¼ teaspoon cayenne
1 pound sea scallops
8 basil leaves

Trim the top and bottom of the fennel bulb, then quarter, lengthwise. Slice the quarters lengthwise into ⅛-inch-thick slices and place in mixing bowl. Toss with 3 tablespoons of the olive oil, 2 tablespoons of the lemon juice, and season to taste with salt and pepper.

In a small saucepan, bring the orange juice, remaining lemon juice, and chili powder to a simmer over medium-high heat. Reduce to ⅓ cup, 15 to 17 minutes. Remove from heat, whisk in the butter, and adjust for salt and pepper if needed.

Mix the flour with cumin and cayenne in a large bowl. Remove the chewy strip on the outside of each scallop and season the scallops with salt and pepper. Add the scallops to the flour mixture and toss to coat well.

Put the remaining oil in a heavy, large skillet over high heat. Sear the scallops until golden brown, about 3 minutes. Turn them over and cook for 3 ½ minutes on the other side. Remove from the pan to drain on paper towels.

To serve, arrange a pile of the sliced fennel salad in a tight circle in the center of six plates. Press to flatten slightly. Arrange the scallops close together on top of the fennel. Drizzle the reduced orange dressing closely around the base of the fennel and over the scallops.

Stack basil leaves and cut lengthwise into julienne strips. Sprinkle on top of scallops.

Scallops are so rich, they are best prepared simply with citrus to cut some of that richness. Almost any citrus will work—lime, lemon, orange, even grapefruit. The crisp fennel acts as a textural contrast. Follow this dish with a roasted chicken, main course salad, or vegetarian entrée. This dish could also be prepared with lobster, shrimp, or crabmeat.

serves 4

With the exception of gazpacho, chilled soups aren't as popular in the United States as they are in the Mediterranean where the summers are long and hot. This soup is perfect for a late summer afternoon lunch when tomatoes are abundant and at their best. Chick peas, always popular in Mediterranean Rim countries, are an ideal thickener for soups like this one. Fortunately, they lose little of their nutty flavor when canned.

chilled chick pea, tomato, and yogurt soup

6 ripe large tomatoes, peeled and seeded (see page 17)
2 tablespoons olive oil
2 cloves garlic, minced
1 teaspoon ground cardamom
1 teaspoon ground cumin
1 teaspoon ground ginger
2 cups canned chick peas, rinsed and drained
1 cup plus ¼ cup plain yogurt
Salt and freshly ground black pepper
12 cilantro leaves, thinly sliced

Chop the tomatoes and set aside. Put the olive oil in a 4-quart saucepan over medium heat. Add the garlic and cook for 2 minutes, stirring to avoid burning. Add the tomatoes, cardamom, cumin, and ginger and cook, uncovered, for 15 minutes, or until the released tomato juices start to thicken.

Transfer the tomato-spice mixture to a food processor or blender and puree. Add the chick peas, ½ cup at a time, pulsing after each addition. The mixture should have a slightly coarse texture. Pour into a bowl, stir in the 1 cup of yogurt, and season with salt and pepper to taste. Refrigerate for at least 1 ½ hours, no more than 48 hours.

To serve, divide the soup among 4 chilled bowls. Place a small dollop of yogurt in the center of each and sprinkle with the cilantro.

baked squash soup with nuts and spices

serves 8

3 tablespoons blanched almonds
3 tablespoons hazelnuts
3 tablespoons sesame seeds
½ teaspoon ground cinnamon
¼ teaspoon ground cloves
1 teaspoon ground ginger
1 teaspoon curry powder
2 pounds butternut squash (1 medium), peeled and cut into ¾-inch cubes (6 cups)
2 tablespoons olive oil
6 cups Chicken Stock (page 15)
1 cup plain yogurt
Salt and freshly ground black pepper
¼ cup chopped cilantro

Preheat the oven to 350 degrees. Put the almonds on a pie plate or small sheet pan and toast for 3 minutes. Add the sesame seeds, keeping them separate from the almonds, and toast for 3 minutes longer. Add the hazelnuts, also keeping them separate, and toast for 11 minutes more, or until the almonds and hazelnuts are browned but not too dark and the sesame seeds are golden. Chop the almonds. Let the hazelnuts cool slightly, rub off the skins in a clean dish towel, and chop. Mix the nuts and sesame seeds and set aside. Raise the oven temperature to 400 degrees.

Combine the cinnamon, cloves, ginger, and curry powder in a small bowl. In a larger mixing bowl toss the squash with the olive oil. Add the spices and mix well. Spread out the squash on a baking sheet.

Bake the squash, covered with aluminum foil, for 20 minutes, or until it softens and the fibers are starting to come apart. Transfer the squash to a large saucepan or stockpot. Add the stock, cover, and bring to a boil over high heat. Reduce the heat and simmer for 15 minutes.

Transfer the squash to a food processor and puree. Strain through a medium-fine strainer, pressing out all the liquid with a wooden spoon or the back of a ladle. Add the yogurt and mix well. Season with salt and pepper to taste.

Divide the soup among warm bowls. Sprinkle with the nut-seed mixture and chopped cilantro.

As fall approaches, hard-shell or winter squash in various colors, shapes, and sizes is a frequent sight in the Mediterranean. Often the squashes grow so large, they're sold by the slice. Winter squash is ideal for soups because it has a naturally creamy texture when pureed with stock. This eliminates the need for cream to enrich (and fatten) the dish. Because winter squash is mild, it's a good idea to enhance the flavor with fragrant spices like cinnamon, cloves, and ginger, as well as nuts and seeds, all of which evoke images of fall and winter.

eggplant puree with yogurt and mint

serves 6 to 8

Roasted and pureed eggplant is ubiquitous in the eastern part of the Mediterranean Rim, served in as many variations as there are cooking styles. Some cooks add tahini, some add yogurt, others just add olive oil—I've even seen anchovies. I use a little of each (except the anchovies), and surround the puree with Spiced Almonds (page 154) and marinated olives and serve it as an hors d'oeuvre. But this puree is much more versatile than that. Try it as a sandwich dressing with grilled lamb or chicken, as a dipping sauce for grilled or raw vegetables, or as a sauce for grilled salmon or sea bass.

2 medium eggplants (about 1 pound each)
1 large clove garlic
2 tablespoons tahini
1 tablespoon plain yogurt
1 tablespoon fresh lemon juice
1 teaspoon ground cumin
¼ cup extra virgin olive oil
Salt and freshly ground black pepper
16 mint leaves, stacked, rolled (if large enough), and cut crosswise into thin strips
¼ cup diced tomato
2 tablespoons chopped parsley
Pita or Flatbread (page 159)

Preheat the oven to 400 degrees. Pierce each eggplant all over with a fork or paring knife and place on a baking sheet. Bake until the skin is charred and the eggplants collapse, 25 to 30 minutes. Or put the eggplants on a charcoal or gas grill 5 inches from the heat source for 13 to 16 minutes, turning every 3 to 4 minutes. Cool, cut in half, and scoop out the flesh.

With the motor running, drop the garlic down the chute of a food processor. When chopped, add the eggplant flesh, tahini, yogurt, lemon juice, cumin, and 3 tablespoons of the oil. Puree until smooth. Season with salt and pepper to taste. Gently fold in the mint.

To serve, place in a decorative bowl. Sprinkle the top with diced tomato, then the chopped parsley. Drizzle with the remaining olive oil. Serve with pita or flatbread for scooping.

portuguese sardines in sweet and sour marinade

serves 8

½ cup fresh lemon juice
½ cup fresh lime juice
½ cup rice vinegar
¼ cup olive oil
¼ cup chopped shallots
½ cup sugar
¼ cup coriander seeds
1 teaspoon crushed red pepper
16 fresh whole sardines, preferably Portuguese type (about 6 ounces each), filleted with the 2 fillets of each sardine left attached
Salt and freshly ground black pepper
20 cilantro leaves

In a medium-size nonreactive saucepan, mix the lemon juice, lime juice, vinegar, 1 tablespoon of the olive oil, the shallots, sugar, coriander seeds, and red pepper. Bring to a boil, reduce the heat, and simmer for 5 minutes. Remove from the heat and let cool.

Heat a heavy skillet, griddle, or broiler to a high temperature. Brush the sardines with the remaining olive oil and season with salt and pepper to taste. Cook, skin side down first, 1 minute per side. Transfer the sardines to a 14 x 10-inch nonreactive (such as glass, enamel, or ceramic) shallow casserole dish to cool.

Pour the marinade over the sardines and add the cilantro leaves. Let stand at room temperature for 1 hour or refrigerate for up to 6 hours.

To serve, remove the sardines from the marinade, place on a large plate, and drizzle with the marinade.

Serve with Almond-Caper Potato Salad (page 45) or a bitter green such as broccoli raab.

Sardines, like anchovies, suffer from the fact that most Americans have never eaten them other than from a can. Fresh sardines are a completely different kettle of fish. I first had them in *pasta con le sarde*, a classic Sicilian dish with wild fennel, currants, pine nuts, and saffron that, more than any other dish I can think of, embodies the flavors of the Mediterranean Rim. If fresh sardines aren't available, substitute small mackerel, brook trout, or smelts.

serves 12

cumin-cured salmon

Salmon is not a Mediterranean fish, but its natural moistness and rich flavor lend themselves to the spices of the Mediterranean Rim. The cumin doesn't overpower the salmon, though the fish is marinated in this strong seasoning for a day or two. Serve this with warm flatbread—either store-bought or homemade (see page 159)—and Tahini-Yogurt Sauce, or plain with a green salad dressed tossed with a light vinaigrette.

2 tablespoons cumin seeds
1 filleted and skinned side of salmon, preferably Atlantic salmon (about 3 to 3 ½ pounds)
¼ cup sea salt or kosher salt
1 ½ tablespoons sugar
1 tablespoon freshly ground black pepper
1 tablespoon ground allspice
Several sprigs cilantro, coarsely chopped
Several sprigs parsley, coarsely chopped
Several sprigs chives, coarsely chopped
3 tablespoons Cognac, or good-quality brandy
1 ½ cups Tahini-Yogurt Sauce (page 158)

Put the cumin seeds in a heavy skillet over medium heat. Toast for 4 minutes, stirring a few times. Grind in a mortar and pestle or a spice grinder. Set aside.

With a needle-nose pliers, remove the small pin bones from the salmon. Place the salmon in a nonreactive (such as glass, enamel, or ceramic) shallow dish.

Combine the cumin, salt, sugar, pepper, and allspice and rub all over the salmon. Spread the herbs on top and sprinkle with Cognac. Wrap tightly with plastic. Put a shallow pan on top of the salmon and weigh it down with cans or something similar. Refrigerate 24 to 48 hours.

To serve, thinly slice on the diagonal. Serve with Tahini-Yogurt Sauce. (The salmon may be refrigerated for up to 2 weeks.)

almond-crusted calamari with mediterranean dipping sauce

serves 6

Deep-fried calamari or squid is often bland with an unappetizing texture. Adding almonds to the batter solves both problems. But to preserve the texture, the heat of the oil is crucial. Too hot, and the almonds will burn. Not hot enough, and the calamari will be soggy and chewy.

¾ cup sliced almonds
¼ cup all-purpose flour
6 cups oil, preferably canola, for deep-frying
½ cup fresh bread crumbs
2 large eggs
2 pounds cleaned squid, bodies cut into ½-inch wide rings, tentacles cut in half
Salt and freshly ground black pepper
2 tablespoons coarsely chopped parsley
1 cup Romesco (page 152) or Tomato Jam (page 153)

Preheat the oven to 350 degrees. Put ½ cup of the sliced almonds on a small sheet pan or pie plate and toast in the oven 8 to 9 minutes, or until browned but not dark. Coarsely chop and set aside. Put the remaining almonds in a food processor with 2 tablespoons of the all-purpose flour. Process until well incorporated. Combine with the remaining flour.

Heat the oil in a large heavy saucepan or deep skillet to 375 degrees.

Mix the chopped almonds with the bread crumbs in a large bowl. Put the flour mixture in a second large bowl, and beat the eggs in a third bowl.

Dip the squid in the flour mixture and shake off any excess. Then dip in the eggs and let any excess liquid drop off. Then roll in the bread crumb mixture to coat well. Shake off excess crumbs and place the squid on wax paper until ready to cook. Repeat until all the squid is coated.

When the oil is ready, add the squid in batches. (To test if the oil is the right temperature without a thermometer, drop a pinch of the bread crumb mixture in the oil. When the mixture sizzles right away, the oil is ready.) Fry the squid 3 to 4 minutes, or until golden brown. Remove with a fine-mesh skimmer or slotted spoon and place on paper towels. Season with salt and pepper to taste, and sprinkle with parsley. Serve in large bowls drizzled with the Romesco or Tomato Jam.

spicy lamb dumplings

serves 6

1 cup all-purpose flour plus extra for dusting
Salt
1 large egg
4 ounces finely ground lean lamb
¼ cup minced onion
1½ tablespoons minced parsley
½ teaspoon salt
¼ teaspoon freshly ground black pepper
½ teaspoon cayenne
⅔ cup plain yogurt, whisked smooth
1½ teaspoons finely crushed dried mint
1 tablespoon finely julienned fresh mint leaves

This is a variation of the classic Turkish dumpling called *manti*. Because of the subtle nature of the sauce, almost any filling can be substituted for lamb—shrimp, beef, chicken, even a vegetarian filling of eggplant or spinach.

In a large bowl, mix the flour and ½ teaspoon salt. Make a well in the center of the mixture. In another bowl, whisk the eggs and 1 tablespoon water. Put the egg mixture into the well of flour, then slowly incorporate the flour into the egg mixture until the two are completely combined.

Lightly dust a work surface with flour and knead the dough until it is smooth and elastic. Let rest, covered with a damp cloth, at room temperature for 30 to 45 minutes.

In a mixing bowl, combine the lamb, onion, parsley, ½ teaspoon salt, ¼ teaspoon black pepper, and ½ teaspoon cayenne. Cover and refrigerate.

Divide the dough into 4 portions. On a floured work surface, roll out each portion as thin as possible, about 1/16 inch thick. Using a 2-inch ring or cookie cutter, cut the dough into circles. Lightly rub the top of each dough circle with cold water. Place ½ teaspoon of the filling in the center. Fold the circle over into a half-moon shape and pinch the edges together in the middle only. Then bring up the two ends of the half-moon to where the dough is pinched, forming a little pouch or purse. Pinch to seal tightly. You should have about 50 dumplings.

Place the dumplings in two 12-inch skillets in 1 layer or cook in 2 batches. Add 1½ cups water to each pan and bring to a boil over high heat. Boil for 4 minutes. (If cooking 2 batches, hold the first batch with its cooking liquid in a heatproof container in an oven set on low heat.)

Divide the yogurt between the 2 pans and simmer over medium-high heat for 1 minute, tossing to coat the dumplings, stirring to incorporate the remaining water into the yogurt. (If working in batches, return the first batch to the skillet and cook both batches in the same skillet for 2 to 3 minutes.) Add the dried mint and adjust for salt and pepper. Serve in bowls sprinkled with fresh mint.

charcoal-grilled beef carpaccio with parmesan-onion salad

serves 4

Strictly speaking, this dish isn't carpaccio—the paper-thin raw beef dish allegedly invented at the Cipriani Hotel in Venice—because the meat is partially cooked, but it has some advantages over the classic carpaccio. First, because the beef is seared, the charred flavor of the meat can tolerate stronger seasoning than if the meat were totally raw. Second, searing firms up the meat to make it easier to slice. To facilitate slicing, carpaccio is usually partially frozen, which I think damages flavor.

1 piece beef fillet (12 ounces), trimmed of all excess fat
2 tablespoons coarsely cracked black peppercorns
½ cup extra virgin olive oil
1 medium sweet onion such as a Vidalia
¼ cup minced chives
2 tablespoons balsamic vinegar
Kosher salt and freshly ground black pepper
8 ounces arugula, tough stems removed
¼ cup fresh lemon juice
1 piece (4 ounces) parmesan, shaved into thin strips with a vegetable peeler

Heat a charcoal grill or a cast-iron skillet over high heat. Spread the cracked peppercorns on a large plate and roll the beef filet in them, coating evenly. Rub the meat with 2 tablespoons of the olive oil or add oil to the skillet. Sear the beef on all sides until well charred, about 2 minutes per side. Refrigerate for 1 to 6 hours.

Peel and quarter the onion. Cut each quarter into ½-inch-wide strips. In a salad bowl, toss the onion, 2 tablespoons of the remaining olive oil, 2 tablespoons of the chives, and the balsamic vinegar. Season with salt and pepper to taste. Set aside.

In a separate bowl, toss the arugula leaves with 2 tablespoons of the lemon juice, 2 tablespoons of the remaining olive oil and salt and pepper to taste. Divide the arugula among 4 plates, arranging it in the center of each plate with the wide parts of the leaves facing outward in a spokelike fashion.

Slice the beef crosswise as thin as possible, no more than ⅛-inch thick. Divide the beef slices evenly among the 4 plates, placing them on top of the arugula. Each plate should have 4 to 6 slices, depending on the size of the fillet and thickness of slices. Place a quarter of the onion salad on top of the beef. Drizzle with the remaining olive oil and lemon juice. Sprinkle with the remaining chives, then with kosher salt, about ¼ teaspoon per plate. Top with the shaved parmesan.

kibbeh with spiced pumpkin

serves 4 to 6

In ***The Cooking of the Eastern Mediterranean*** **author Paula Wolfert calls kibbeh "one of the most interesting forms of ground meat cookery" because it is so varied with different nuts and spices and because it is cooked in so many ways. While kibbeh is traditionally made with lamb, it can also be made with beef, veal, rabbit, even turkey. This Lebanese version is served with Tahini-Yogurt Sauce.**

¼ cup blanched almonds
2 tablespoons cumin seeds
1 tablespoon Spicy Olive Oil (page 13)
¼ cup chopped onion
12 ounces ground lamb
2 ½ tablespoons ground allspice
2 cloves garlic, minced
¼ cup defrosted, drained, and chopped frozen leaf spinach
¼ cup cooked (canned or fresh) chick peas
2 tablespoons fresh lemon juice
Salt
Cayenne
1 cup canned pumpkin puree (not pie filling)
1 teaspoon honey
2 cups medium-grind bulgur
⅓ cup all-purpose flour
1 shallot, grated
Freshly ground black pepper, to taste
Olive oil
4 cups canola oil for frying
1 ½ cups Tahini-Yogurt Sauce (page 158)

Preheat the oven to 350 degrees. Put the almonds on a small sheet pan or pie plate and toast for 17 minutes, or until browned but not too dark. Cool to room temperature, chop, and set aside. Meanwhile, put the cumin seeds in a heavy skillet over medium heat. Toast for 4 minutes, stirring a few times. Grind with a mortar and pestle or in a spice grinder.

Put the Spicy Olive Oil in a medium skillet over medium-high heat. Add the onion and sauté 3 to 4 minutes, or until somewhat translucent. Add the lamb, allspice, and garlic and cook, stirring until the lamb turns color from red to brown. Add the almonds, spinach, chick peas, lemon juice, and salt and cayenne to taste. Scrape into a mixing bowl.

In another mixing bowl, mix the pumpkin, honey, bulgur, flour, shallot, and cumin seeds. Season with salt and cayenne to taste. Remove from the bowl and knead gently to incorporate the ingredients until the mixture holds together.

Fill a third bowl with cold water and 1 tablespoon salt for keeping hands moist. As the pumpkin mixture begins to dry, its surface will look dull. Add a few drops of water to keep moist. Wet your fingertips and palms and between your palms and cupped fingers, roll 2 tablespoons of the pumpkin mixture into an oval shape, like a semi-flattened egg, about 1 inch thick. Hold in the cup of one hand and poke a hole in the middle with your forefinger or the narrow end of a wooden spoon. Insert 1 teaspoon of the lamb mixture into the opening. Seal the open end and roll between your cupped hands to seal tightly. Brush with olive oil and refrigerate, covered, until ready to cook. You should have 22 to 26 kibbeh.

In a deep, iron skillet, heat the canola oil to 375 degrees. (Or test by dropping in a small piece of one kibbeh. If the oil sizzles immediately, it's ready.) Fry the kibbeh five at a time until golden brown, 1½ to 2 minutes. Drain on paper towels. Serve hot or at room temperature with Tahini-Yogurt Sauce.

crostini of wild mushrooms with cardamom

serves 4

Grilled slices of country bread, called bruschetta, are common in Italy, especially Tuscany. They are prepared with simple, rustic toppings, often not more than brush of olive oil and a rub of cut garlic. When the slices are smaller, they are called crostini and the toppings become more refined. The following is my take on crostini, using a walnut bread. Any good sourdough bread will also do.

¼ cup hazelnuts
1 ½ pounds wild mushrooms such as chanterelles, shiitakes, trumpets, and porcini
3 tablespoons unsalted butter
1 ½ teaspoons ground cardamom
¼ cup port or madeira
2 teaspoons chopped parsley
Salt and freshly ground black pepper
4 slices walnut bread, ½-inch-thick, toasted or grilled
4 sprigs fresh thyme

Preheat the oven to 350 degrees. Put the hazelnuts on a small sheet pan or pie plate and toast for 11 minutes, or until browned but not dark. Wrap the nuts in a clean dish towel and rub off skins. Chop and set aside.

Remove any tough stems from the mushrooms (such as those on shiitakes) and discard. Cut mushrooms into uniform pieces, about 1 inch long and ½ inch thick.

Heat the butter in a large skillet over medium-high heat until it stops sizzling. Add the mushrooms and reduce the heat to medium. Cook for 6 to 8 minutes, or until the mushrooms are visibly shrunken and glossy. Add the cardamom and hazelnuts and cook for another 3 minutes. Add the port and parsley, toss, and cook 1 to 2 minutes more, or until the mushrooms are slightly glazed. Season with salt and pepper to taste.

Cut each slice of toast into quarters and overlap the quarters on each of 4 plates. Spoon the warm mushrooms over the toast and garnish with the thyme sprigs on the side.

salads

The concept of salads along the Mediterranean Rim is much broader and more flexible than what many Americans are used to. One reason is that salads can be found in almost any part of the meal or as the meal itself. By contrast, the salad has long been a minor player at the very beginning of an American meal—though that is changing. Another reason is that the ingredients that go into a salad are more varied. Virtually any vegetable from carrots to cauliflower can be part of a salad. Grains like bulgur and rice are also used extensively in salads, such as the Sicilian-Style Rice Salad with Tuna and Mint and the Bulgur with Fava Beans (page 63). The grainlike couscous is also used in salad, as in the Tunisian Couscous Salad. When you add great flavor enhancers like toasted nuts, olives, and capers you are assured of an almost unlimited variety of tastes, colors, and textures.

Chopped Summer Salad with Feta, Favas, and Green Onions

Produce, especially vegetables, is still a major component of salads. That requires finding the freshest, highest quality ingredients possible. As with seafood, it's hard to hide inferior ingredients in salads. I cringe when I see people buying tomatoes in January. Tomatoes are enjoyable in salads, but I use only locally grown tomatoes—they're the only ones that have any taste. If they're available only in summer or early fall, so be it. And since tomatoes are a tropical fruit, I never refrigerate them, for their flavor would be severely damaged. Instead, I store tomatoes at cool room temperature, about 65 degrees.

It's almost axiomatic to say that salad greens should be completely dry before dressing is added, but you might be surprised at how many people—even restaurants—fail to do this. The result is a salad whose dressing doesn't cling to the ingredients but falls to the bottom of the bowl. Salad greens should be spun dry in a salad spinner, then covered with a clean, damp dish towel or paper towels, and refrigerated until needed.

While Americans have used raw vegetables in salads, cooked vegetables are being seen more frequently. In many cases they actually work better. I'm not particularly fond of raw cauliflower, broccoli, or green beans in salads, but cooked, they're great. This requires blanching the vegetables in lots of salted water, then chilling or "shocking" them in ice water to stop the cooking and retain color. You still want some crunch, though, so don't cook the vegetables too far. As with salad greens, they should be well drained of moisture.

Bathed in a flavorful vinaigrette, cooked vegetables can be terrific. But when made ahead and refrigerated, they may taste of the refrigerator. If you must make such a salad ahead of time, cover it tightly so it doesn't pick up any flavors from the refrigerator. Then bring it to room temperature at least 30 minutes before serving. My preference, however, is to keep such salads at room temperature on ice.

Because fruit is abundant along the Mediterranean Rim, fruit salads are common. Unlike many fruit salads we're used to in the United States, Mediterranean fruit salads are often savory salads that contain meats, cheese, olives, and other full-flavored ingredients. The juice in the fruit also acts as an acid and decreases the reliance on vinegar. Thus you have in this chapter a Spiced Venison Salad with Blood Orange Marinade as well as Bitter Greens with Walnut Dressing, Blue Cheese, and Figs.

As for nonproduce salad ingredients, the sky's the limit as far as I'm concerned, from bread—as in the Chopped Summer Salad with Feta, Favas, and Green Onions, which contains grilled pita; and Tomato and Sourdough Bread Salad with Capers—to nuts and olives, as in my Almond-Caper Potato Salad or Red Lettuces with Almonds, Green Olives, and Manchego Cheese.

I enjoy cheeses in salads such as Spanish manchego and cabrales. Other good cheeses to add to salads include Italian parmesan (the real thing, Parmigiano-Reggiano), pecorino, fresh mozzarella, feta, and goat cheese. The rule I follow when adding cheese to salads is to shave or grate strongly flavored, hard cheeses like parmesan so you don't get a big chunk in your mouth. Milder, softer cheeses can be cubed or left in larger pieces. Feta, which can be sharp or creamy depending on where it is made, is usually cut into small pieces or crumbled over the top.

The accepted ratio of acid to oil in salad dressing used to be one part acid (lemon juice or vinegar) to three, even four parts oil. As we Americans have become more health conscious, that ratio has changed to perhaps two parts acid to three parts oil and sometimes one to one. I've even seen some customers in my restaurant order a dry salad and sprinkle on nothing but balsamic vinegar.

New vinegars with lower acid levels make it possible to reduce the amount of oil in dressings without having the dressings taste vinegary. For example, fruit vinegars such as those from Consorzio are as low as 4 percent acid, compared to many other vinegars that are 5, 6, or 7 percent acid (though I must admit, many of the fruit vinegars out today are a little too tropical for my taste.)

Balsamic vinegars have a richness and sweetness that make them more palatable than many harsher wine vinegars. I also like red wine and sherry vinegars because they have a more rounded flavor than white wine vinegar, which to me is just a straight shot of acid without much complexity.

I vary the type of salad dressing depending on the time of year. In summer, I favor lemon juice (always freshly squeezed) with fruity olive oils. Other citrus juices like clementine or blood orange juice would have the same effect. As fall approaches, I switch the acid in my dressing to a balsamic, sherry, or red wine vinegar or mix one of them with an equal amount of lemon juice. Also, because fall makes me think more about nuts, I put nut oils like almond, walnut, and hazelnut oil into my dressings.

Stronger salad ingredients can tolerate stronger dressings. For example, with bitter greens like endive, radicchio, and arugula, a stronger wine vinegar and more peppery olive oil can often be used. Or it may be a combination of wine vinegar and lemon juice with a flavorful walnut oil as in the Bitter Greens with Walnut Dressing, Blue Cheese, and Figs. In addition, you can sometimes add a more pungent seasoning like garlic as I do in the Chopped Summer Salad with Feta, Favas, and Green Onions. Conversely, such a dressing would overwhelm more delicate ingredients like red leaf or Boston lettuce, mild cheeses, and many fruits.

I wouldn't dream of a summer salad without fresh mint or basil because of the clean flavors they add. Summer basil, however, is a whole different world from the insipid herb we see in winter. When basil is out of season, I resort to chives and parsley, especially Italian flat-leaf parsley, which is more robust than curly parsley. Not all fresh herbs are appropriate for salads, though. Rosemary and sage, for example, are too strong. I never use dried herbs in salads.

When you assemble a salad, keep in mind that more is not always better. If you have too many ingredients, individual flavors get lost. On the other hand, you can make a splendid salad with just one or two ingredients like perfectly ripe tomatoes from the backyard and sweet red onions. You also don't want to have too many strong flavors competing, even if the total number of ingredients isn't high. For example, a salad with olives, anchovies, capers, and cheese would have too much salt.

Finally, I think a salad should be easy and enjoyable to eat and not an obstacle course. Big pieces of lettuce or vegetables are cumbersome and silly. That's why I favor salads with chopped or diced ingredients as in the Chopped Summer Salad with Feta, Favas, and Green Onions. In addition to being easier to eat, such salads allow a much faster penetration of dressing, which means less dressing is needed.

Tunisian Couscous Salad

tunisian couscous salad

serves 4

3 medium red bell peppers
1 ½ cups instant couscous (10 ounces)
Salt
¼ cup olive oil
¼ cup fresh lemon juice
1 teaspoon ground cumin
Freshly ground black pepper
Cayenne
1 large English (hothouse) cucumber, peeled and cut into ½-inch dice
½ cup Moroccan or other small, black, oil-cured olives, pitted and coarsely chopped
2 green onions, white parts and about 3 inches of green parts, minced
1 large clove garlic, minced
1 pound ripe beefsteak tomatoes, peeled, seeded, and cut into ½-inch dice (see page 17)
2 tablespoons finely chopped parsley

Preheat the broiler. Put the peppers on a sheet pan lined with foil and broil for about 15 minutes, turning once or twice to ensure they blister and blacken evenly. Remove to a bowl, cover with plastic wrap, and let cool. Peel, seed, and cut into ½-inch dice. Set aside.

Put the couscous in a large mixing bowl. Pour 2¼ cups boiling water over the couscous. Add ½ teaspoon salt and stir. Cover with plastic wrap, and let stand for 10 to 15 minutes, or until swollen and tender.

In a small bowl, combine the olive oil, lemon juice, and cumin. Season with salt, pepper, and cayenne to taste.

Fluff the couscous with a fork. Add the cucumber, olives, green onions, garlic, tomatoes, and roasted peppers. Pour the dressing over the couscous and toss to combine. Let stand at room temperature for at least 1 hour. Just before serving, stir in the parsley.

Even though I call this salad Tunisian, the ingredients could put it in several countries of North Africa. The only thing you have to be concerned about in this dish is overcooking the couscous by pouring on too much boiling water. Otherwise, this salad is very forgiving. It allows you to adjust seasonings and substitute other ingredients almost at will. Chopped grilled vegetables, sautéed mushrooms, and grilled or poached chicken are just a few of the ingredients that can be added to this salad, which is easily transformed into a main course. Like the Sicilian-Style Rice Salad with Tuna and Mint (page 48) and the Bulgur with Fava Beans (page 63), it's a good choice for a picnic or buffet.

chopped summer salad with feta, favas, and green onions

serves 6

I love this refreshing salad on hot, humid summer evenings in New York. It's an excellent meal starter, like a Greek salad, but it can also be a meal in itself. Ingredients are extremely flexible. Vegetables can be raw, cooked, or a combination of the two. Firmer vegetables like carrots, green beans and asparagus should be cooked. Watery vegetables like cucumbers should be raw. Leftover vegetables are also good and so are beans like chick peas. A tangy goat cheese can be used instead of feta. The simple dressing can be enlivened with a spicy or flavored oil. Balsamic vinegar can be substituted for lemon juice.

½ pound fava beans, shelled (about ½ cup)
Salt
1 large red bell pepper
1 large Greek (pocketless) pita (about 10 to 12 inches in diameter)
½ cup plus 1 teaspoon olive oil plus additional for drizzling, if desired
1 clove garlic, minced
¼ cup chopped parsley
¼ cup chopped mint leaves
¼ cup chopped basil leaves
⅓ cup fresh lemon juice
1 cup finely chopped inner leaves of romaine lettuce
1 large cucumber, peeled, seeded, and chopped
2 ripe small beefsteak tomatoes, seeded and diced (see page 17)
½ cup chopped green onions, white parts and green parts up to 1 inch from the top
Freshly ground black pepper
⅔ cup crumbled feta (about 4 ounces)

Cook the fava beans in a quart of boiling, salted water for 3 minutes. Drain. When cooled, peel the beans by tearing off a small piece of skin the from the rounded end with your fingernail. Squirt out the beans by pinching the opposite end. Set aside.

Preheat the broiler. Put the pepper on a sheet pan lined with foil and broil for about 15 minutes, turning once or twice to ensure it blisters and blackens evenly. Remove to a bowl, cover with plastic wrap, and let cool. Peel, seed, and dice. Set aside.

Meanwhile, brush the pita with 1 teaspoon of the olive oil. Broil about 5 inches from the heat source for about 3 minutes per side, or until edges begin to curl and the bread becomes firm. Sprinkle with a pinch of salt and let cool for 5 to 7 minutes. Break the pita into ½-inch pieces.

In a small bowl, mix the garlic, parsley, mint, basil, and lemon juice. Slowly whisk in ½ cup of the olive oil.

In a large, colorful salad bowl, mix the romaine, cucumber, tomatoes, bell pepper, green onions, and fava beans. Add the dressing and toss well. Add the pita and toss again. Season with salt and pepper. Serve topped with crumbled feta and a drizzle of olive oil, if desired.

tomato and sourdough bread salad with capers

serves 4

8 slices (1 ½ inches thick) stale sourdough bread (1 ¼ pounds)
24 basil leaves
¾ cup extra virgin olive oil
3 tablespoons red wine vinegar
1 medium sweet onion such as Vidalia, halved and thinly sliced
4 ripe medium tomatoes, peeled, seeded, and chopped (see page 17)
6 tablespoons capers, drained
Salt and freshly ground black pepper

In a large bowl, break the bread into large pieces, about 2 to 3 inches. Pour 3 cups cold water over the bread, toss, and let soak for 6 to 8 minutes, gently tossing again after 3 or 4 minutes. Squeeze the bread to remove the water. Break into 1-inch pieces and put in a clean bowl.

Stack 16 of the basil leaves, roll like a cigar, and cut crosswise into thin strips. Add ½ cup of the olive oil and 2 tablespoons of the vinegar to the bread. Add the basil strips, onion, tomatoes, and capers. Season with salt and pepper to taste. Mix well. Refrigerate for 1 to 2 hours and adjust the seasoning, adding more vinegar, salt, and pepper, if desired.

Divide the salad among 4 shallow bowls. Drizzle with the remaining olive oil and garnish with the remaining basil leaves and, if desired, additional black pepper.

This variation of panzanella, the classic Tuscan bread salad, is given a Sicilian twist with the addition of piquant capers. Good, dense sourdough bread is essential in this recipe for two reasons. First, its firm texture can stand soaking in water, then the liquid from tomatoes, olive oil, and vinegar without falling apart. Second, the tangy sourdough bread holds up to the flavors of the olive oil, basil, and tomatoes, as well as the briny capers. Obviously, this is a summer salad, best when tomatoes and basil are at their peak.

fennel salad with clementines and moroccan olives

serves 4

This dish is traditionally made with oranges, but I prefer the sweeter clementines we see in winter, imported from Spain and Morocco in those cute little wooden crates. Shiny, jet black oil-cured Moroccan olives offer a nice color contrast as well as a salty counterpoint to the clementines. This is a good finish to a heavy meal or it can be used as part of a mezze table.

5 teaspoons anise seeds
Juice of 4 clementines or 2 juice oranges
1 tablespoon minced onion or shallot
¼ cup extra virgin olive oil
2 small bulbs fennel
10 clementines or 5 navel oranges, peeled with membranes or white pith removed, and sectioned
24 black Moroccan or other black oil-cured olives, pitted
1 tablespoon chopped chives
½ cup (loosely packed) arugula leaves, washed and dried
Salt and freshly ground black pepper

Put the anise seeds in a heavy skillet over medium heat. Toast for 4 minutes, stirring a few times. Grind 2½ teaspoons of the seeds with a mortar and pestle. Set ground and whole toasted seeds aside separately.

Combine the clementine juice, onion, and ground anise seeds in a small bowl. Slowly whisk in the olive oil. Set aside.

Remove green tops from fennel and discard. Cut the bulbs lengthwise in half and cut out the firm center core. Cut lengthwise into strips, about ⅛ inch wide.

Place the fennel, clementines, olives, chives, and arugula in a large bowl and toss with the dressing. Season with salt and pepper to taste. Divide the salad among 4 plates. Sprinkle with the reserved whole anise seeds.

Serve with Braised Lamb Shank with Dried Apricots (page 105) or Lamb Tagine with Dried Figs and Almonds (page 108).

serves 4

Figs have grown in great profusion all along the Mediterranean Rim for thousands of years. In this salad, with cheese and nuts, they produce a fairly filling dish, which can be a light meal on its own. When used as an appetizer, match it with a light main course such as a grilled or broiled fish or chicken.

bitter greens with walnut dressing, blue cheese, and figs

2/3 cup walnuts
1/4 cup fresh lemon juice
2 tablespoons sherry vinegar or red wine vinegar
1 egg (see Note)
1/2 cup walnut oil
Salt and freshly ground black pepper
2 heads Belgian endive
2 small heads radicchio
1 bunch (8 ounces) arugula, tough stems removed
3/4 cup crumbled cabrales or other quality blue cheese such as gorgonzola
8 fresh, ripe Mission figs, trimmed and quartered lengthwise
1/3 cup minced chives

Preheat the oven to 350 degrees. Put the walnuts on a small sheet pan or pie plate and toast for 13 minutes, or until they smell nutty and are darker (but not too dark). Coarsely chop and set aside.

Mix the lemon juice, vinegar, and egg in a small mixing bowl. Slowly whisk in the walnut oil and season with salt and pepper to taste. Set aside.

Separate the leaves of the Belgian endive. Stack one on top of the other, then cut crosswise into 1-inch-wide strips. Remove any outer damaged leaves from the radicchio. Cut in half, remove the inner core, then cut each half into quarters. Separate the leaves. In a large salad bowl, mix the endive and radicchio with the arugula. Add the walnuts and 1/2 cup of the cabrales. Add about half of the dressing and gently toss. Taste and add more dressing as desired. Recheck the seasoning.

Arrange the fig quarters in a circle around the perimeter of the salad. Sprinkle the top with the remaining cheese and sprinkle with chives.

NOTE In recent years, some outbreaks of salmonella have been traced to raw eggs. If you are concerned about the safety of the eggs in your area, make this salad dressing without the eggs. It will not coat as well but the flavor will be fine.

Serve with Flatbread (page 159) or toasted pita.

almond-caper potato salad

serves 4

¼ cup blanched whole almonds
1 pound new potatoes, Ping-Pong ball size, scrubbed but not peeled
Salt
4 green onions, white parts and two thirds of the green parts, minced
4 teaspoons small capers, drained
16 large mint leaves, stacked, rolled like a cigar, and cut crosswise into thin strips
12 basil leaves, stacked, rolled like a cigar, and cut crosswise into thin strips
¼ cup extra virgin olive oil
2 tablespoons sherry vinegar or red wine vinegar
1 tablespoon fresh lemon juice
¼ teaspoon crushed red pepper
Freshly ground black pepper

Preheat the oven to 350 degrees. Put the almonds on a small sheet pan or pie plate and toast for 17 minutes, or until browned but not too dark. Coarsely chop and set aside.

Meanwhile, put the potatoes in a large saucepan with 2 quarts cold water and 1 tablespoon salt. Bring to a boil over high heat, reduce the heat, and simmer for 20 to 25 minutes, or until tender. Drain.

Quarter the potatoes lengthwise while still warm and put into a large bowl. Add the green onions, capers, almonds, mint, and basil. In a small bowl, mix the oil, vinegar, and lemon juice with the crushed red pepper. Season with salt and black pepper to taste. Pour over the potato mixture and mix well. Allow to cool to room temperature.

Serve with any grilled fish or meat or other simple entree.

Potato salad may seem as American as the Fourth of July, but this one gets a real Mediterranean Rim treatment with almonds, capers, basil, and mint. Just because a potato is small or red-skinned doesn't mean it's "new." New potatoes are freshly dug up and have thin skins that can literally be rubbed off. That means you don't have to peel them. And because they're closer to their natural state, they taste better.

red lettuces with spiced almonds, green olives, and manchego cheese

serves 4

1 shallot, minced
3 tablespoons fresh lemon juice
¼ cup chopped chives
½ teaspoon freshly ground black pepper
Salt
⅓ cup almond, walnut, or hazelnut oil
8 ounces cleaned red lettuces such as red romaine, lollo rossa, red oak leaf, and radicchio (about 12 cups)
½ cup grated parmesan
32 green olives, preferably picholine, pitted
½ cup Spiced Almonds (page 154)
8 thin slices manchego or asiago

In a small mixing bowl, whisk together the shallot, lemon juice, chives, pepper, and salt to taste. Slowly whisk in the almond oil. Set aside.

Put the lettuces, parmesan, olives, and almonds in a large salad bowl. Toss to combine. Add the dressing and toss to dress thoroughly. Readjust seasoning, if desired.

Divide the lettuce among 4 salad plates. Be sure the olives and almonds are evenly divided. Lean 2 slices of the manchego against each of the salads.

Olives are great for salads because they don't need to be cooked, they're densely flavored, and they don't break down under dressing. I prefer the smallish, green picholine olives from southern France because I like their sweetness and firm texture, but good small green olives from Greece, Italy, or Spain will do.

sicilian-style rice salad with tuna and mint

serves 4

This dish is different from most rice salads in that it uses Arborio rice, which has a creamy texture even though it isn't constantly stirred as it is in risotto. Because it is more glutinous than long-grain rice, Arborio pulls flavors together rather than leaving them separate, the way they are in most rice salads. Follow this basic method and make something special from leftover shrimp, chicken, or vegetables by substituting them for the tuna. Stirring in a pesto, Romesco (page 152), or Middle Eastern Salsa Verde (page 151) will further enhance the flavor.

1 teaspoon saffron threads
2 cups Arborio rice
Salt
2 cans (6 ounces each) albacore tuna packed in olive oil
⅓ cup extra virgin olive oil, if using tuna other than olive oil–packed
1 ½ pounds (about 10) ripe plum tomatoes, peeled, seeded, and chopped (see page 17)
2 tablespoons small capers, drained
1 red onion, finely chopped
2 tablespoons fresh lemon juice
¼ teaspoon crushed red pepper
¼ cup thinly sliced mint leaves plus 8 whole mint leaves for garnish
Freshly ground black pepper

Bring 4½ cups water to a boil with the saffron in a medium saucepan over medium-high heat. Reduce the heat slightly and simmer for 10 minutes. Add the rice and 1 teaspoon of salt and stir. Cook, covered, for 20 to 25 minutes, or until the liquid is absorbed and the rice is tender. Transfer the rice to a bowl and let it cool.

Put the tuna and its oil in a large salad bowl. Add the ⅓ cup of olive oil, if needed, and gently mix in the tomatoes, capers, onion, lemon juice, red pepper, and sliced mint. Add the cooked rice and mix well. Season with salt and black pepper. Let stand at room temperature for at least 1 hour before serving.

Serve the salad in a large decorative bowl garnished with mint leaves.

Serve as a side dish with a sandwich, with grilled or roasted vegetables, or as part of a mezze table or antipasto platter.

spiced venison salad with blood orange marinade

serves 6

4 green onions, white parts and 1½ inches of green parts, chopped
1 medium onion, chopped
1 clove garlic, chopped
½ teaspoon ground allspice
1 ¼ cups blood orange juice or plain fresh orange juice
2 tablespoons honey
2 tablespoons sherry vinegar
1 ½ pounds loin of venison, cut into three 8-ounce steaks
4 teaspoons pine nuts
½ cup olive oil
1 tablespoon grated orange zest
1 blood orange or navel orange, peeled with pith and seeds removed, and sectioned
Salt and freshly ground black pepper
2 bunches arugula (about1 pound), tough stems removed
2 tablespoons chopped chives

Puree the green onions, onion, garlic, and allspice in a food processor. Add 1 cup of the juice, 1 tablespoon of the honey and 1 tablespoon of the vinegar. Blend well. Fit the meat tightly in a casserole or baking dish and pour the marinade over. Coat well by turning the meat, then cover with plastic wrap. Refrigerate for 6 to 24 hours.

Preheat the oven to 350 degrees. Put the pine nuts on a small sheet pan or pie plate and toast for 9 to 10 minutes, or until golden brown. Remove and let cool. Increase the oven temperature to 450 degrees.

In a mixing bowl, combine ¼ cup of the olive oil, the orange zest, orange sections, the remaining 1 tablespoon honey, the remaining 1 tablespoon vinegar and pine nuts. Season with salt and pepper. Set aside.

Put the remaining ¼ cup olive oil in a medium ovenproof skillet over high heat. Brush excess marinade from the venison, season with salt and pepper, and brown on all sides, 6 minutes total. Put the skillet in the oven and cook for 4 minutes. The meat should be done no more than medium rare. Remove the meat from the skillet and transfer to a cutting board to rest for 3 to 4 minutes.

Toss the arugula with the dressing and divide among 6 plates. Cut each steak into thin slices, about ¼ inch thick. You should have about 24 slices, or 4 per serving. Arrange the meat over the arugula. Sprinkle with chives and pepper. Drizzle any orange dressing left in the bowl over the salads.

Blood oranges are a common sight in the Mediterranean, and they are becoming more available in the United States—mostly from California, though some are imported. Venison, like most other game, works well in hearty salads because it is very lean. Also like other game, venison can handle the kind of sweetness this dish has without being cloying.

risotto, grains, and pasta

The most appealing aspect of grain dishes is that they allow you to put your own individual stamp on them. We've all heard people brag about their mom's pasta sauce, but those boasts have expanded in recent years. Now I have customers tell me about drop-dead risottos they or their friends make.

Risotto was one of the major influences on my decision to become a chef. The first time I tasted it, at Elio's restaurant in New York, I thought the chef must have some magical powers. I had grown up eating plain old white rice. Consequently, rice that combined the flavors of earthy mushrooms, sharp parmesan, rich chicken stock, and fresh herbs—all in one dish—was something new and wonderful. When made well, risotto acts like a symphony, combining the music of many instruments into one clear and delicious composition.

Curried Shellfish Risotto

The key to great risotto is the proper rice. The kind to use is a special medium-grain rice that releases starch as it gently cooks in stock. This creates risotto's creamy texture so effectively that you could eliminate cheese or butter if you had to. There are three main varieties on the market: Arborio, Carnaroli, and Vialone Nano, all of which are imported from Italy, though U.S. growers are beginning to produce domestic versions. I use Vialone Nano because it holds up better under restaurant conditions, but for home use any good Arborio, the most commonly available of the three rices, is fine.

I've used other grains for risotto-like dishes such as Toasted Barley Risotto with Wild Mushrooms. Barley retains its texture during cooking and assimilates flavors much like rice suitable for risotto, though it doesn't provide the creaminess. Though there is no recipe for it in this book, I've also used basmati rice in risotto to add an element from the eastern part of the Mediterranean Rim. But again, it doesn't act entirely like normal risotto rice.

The quality of the stock is also important in risotto. Most often chicken stock is used, though seafood and vegetable stocks are also suitable. Stir the risotto regularly with a wooden spoon that has a flat edge to scrape the entire bottom of the pan, so the risotto doesn't get dry while it cooks. A few other points when making risotto: Purees like pesto should be added at the end of the cooking process. Added too early, they will adversely change the consistency. The same is true for cheese, which makes the risotto gluey if added too soon.

While risotto can contain nothing much more than chopped onion, it is a dish that begs to be a vehicle for many ingredients, much like pasta. Seasonal vegetables are a natural: asparagus in the spring; corn and tomatoes in summer (as in White Corn Risotto with Pancetta, Tomatoes, and Pine Nuts); and wild mushrooms in the fall. I also like risotto with shellfish, particularly shrimp and scallops as in my Curried Shellfish Risotto.

As for other kinds of rice, basmati makes a terrific side dish by itself because if its nutty aroma and sweet flavor. It also lends itself to preparations like pancakes, where the rice is boiled and fried (as in the Basmati Pancake with Saffron, Honey, and Mint), and to pilafs where the rice is steamed with other ingredients, such as Basmati Rice with Eggplant, Almonds, and Basil. Most basmati is imported from India, but domestic versions such as Texmati can be quite good, though they're usually not as fragrant. I've also had success with specialty rices like the black japonica and Wehani now on the market.

Though technically a pasta, couscous is often considered a grain. It's popular along the southern Mediterranean Rim, in North Africa and especially in Morocco. Couscous can be prepared in one of two ways. In the more traditional way, the couscous is put in a steamer. Moroccans use a two-part pot called a couscoussière, but a satisfactory alternative is to put any type of colander with small holes over a pot. The procedure is described in Couscous with Chicken, Almonds, and Squash (page 64). In this method, the aroma and flavor of the stew permeate the couscous, which sits above it.

In the second method, boiling liquid is poured over the couscous in a bowl, which is then covered. The couscous soaks up the liquid and steams at the same time. This procedure is most often employed when the couscous will be used in salad as in the Tunisian Couscous Salad (page 39). The combinations of couscous salad you can make are as varied as any pasta salad.

Bulgur, nutty crushed wheat kernels, is usually soaked like couscous for salads, as in Bulgur with Fava Beans. It can also be used as a hot grain like rice, sometimes mixed with rice or other grains in a pilaf. Bulgur is now widely available in supermarkets. You can also find it in different size grinds at Middle Eastern markets and other specialty stores. The finest grind is traditionally used in the most popular bulgur dish, tabbouleh.

Pasta has been so warmly embraced in this country, we almost think of it as American. I'd like to make two cautionary points, however. First, many people get so hung up about making sure the pasta is firm or al dente that they undercook it. But undercooked pasta won't combine well with the other ingredients of a dish, particularly the sauce. I like my pasta firm, but cooked through, with a minuscule spot of white still showing at the very center when the pasta is broken in two.

Second is the distinction between dried and fresh pasta. For a while, it was assumed that fresh pasta was superior to dried pasta, but I have found the contrary is often true. Fresh pasta overcooks quickly and can be gluey or mushy. It's also more expensive than dried pasta, and good-quality fresh pasta is not always readily available. So unless you're making ravioli or some other stuffed pasta, stick with the dried.

I use DeCecco brand dried Italian pasta, but many other reliable brands of pasta are imported from Italy. Good-quality dried pasta will hold up even if cooked a minute or two longer than you intended. And it offers a seemingly unlimited number of shapes and sizes to choose from, which makes cooking pasta a lot of fun.

Seasonal vegetables always inspire me to make pasta dishes, whether they're fresh beans, tomatoes, or basil in summer, broccoli raab or mushrooms in winter, or sweet peas or asparagus in spring. A well-stocked pantry with items like jarred roasted peppers, canned beans, sun-dried tomatoes, good oil, crushed red pepper, and garlic enables you to put together some fine pasta meals all year round.

white corn risotto with pancetta, tomato, and pine nuts

serves 4

¼ cup pine nuts
8 ½ cups Chicken Stock (page 15)
1 teaspoon saffron threads
¼ cup extra virgin olive oil
2 ounces pancetta or bacon, diced (about ¼ cup)
½ medium onion, chopped
2 cups Arborio rice
1 cup dry white wine
6 plum tomatoes, peeled, halved, and seeded (see page 17), each cut lengthwise into 4 strips
3 cups fresh white corn kernels (about 6 ears)
1 tablespoon unsalted butter
⅓ cup grated parmesan plus additional cheese for the table
Salt and fresh ground black pepper
¼ cup thinly sliced basil leaves

Preheat the oven to 350 degrees. Put the pine nuts on a pie plate or small sheet pan and toast for 9 to 10 minutes, or until golden brown. Set aside.

In a large saucepan, bring the stock to a boil with the saffron threads. Reduce the heat and simmer, uncovered, for 20 minutes. Strain through a fine mesh strainer and keep warm.

Put the olive oil in a medium-size heavy saucepan over medium-high heat. Add the pancetta and cook for 3 to 4 minutes. Pour out half of the fat, add the onion and cook for 3 to 4 minutes, or until the onion begins to soften. Add the rice, stirring with a wooden spoon until coated with fat, about 30 seconds.

Add the wine and allow it to evaporate, about 3 minutes. Add 2 cups of the warm saffron stock, stir and allow the liquid to be absorbed while stirring periodically. Continue adding stock, 1 cup at a time, as each preceding cup is absorbed. Add the last cup of warm stock, if needed, and continue stirring until the rice has a creamy but not runny texture. Cooking time from the first addition of stock, is 23 to 26 minutes. Stir in the pine nuts, tomatoes, corn, butter, and parmesan.

Season with salt and pepper to taste and stir in the basil. Serve in large bowls with additional parmesan on top, if desired.

The marriage of corn and tomatoes captures the essence of August in America. I also like the combination of corn and bacon. By putting all three together (with pancetta instead of bacon for a Mediterranean touch) I get an earthy summer flavor. Without the rice, the corn, tomatoes, and pancetta would make a fine summer vegetable ragout, a succotash (with some fresh or frozen lima beans), warm salad, or even a pasta sauce.

serves 4

Curry is considered a flavor of the Mediterranean Rim, but curry powder—a blend which usually includes turmeric, cumin, cardamom, cayenne, and sometimes coriander and cinnamon—is not far from *ras el hanout*, the combination of spices popular in Morocco. While Indians and Moroccans would always make their spice blends from scratch, a commercial curry powder is fine for this recipe. The only caveat is that the curry be added early in the cooking. This mellows out the harshness that the curry would have if added later, and gives it time to permeate the other elements in the dish. Putting the curry over direct heat, as opposed to dissolving it in liquid, also gives it a toasted flavor.

curried shellfish risotto

½ cup olive oil
1 medium onion, finely chopped
2 cloves garlic, minced
2 ½ tablespoons high-quality curry powder such as Madras
¼ teaspoon ground dried chilies such as ancho, or chili powder
2 cups Arborio rice
1 cup dry white wine
8 cups warm Shellfish or Chicken Stock (pages 16 and 15)
¼ pound cleaned squid bodies, cut into ⅛-inch-wide rings
½ pound bay scallops, or sea scallops cut in half
¼ pound medium-large shrimp (4 to 5), shelled and deveined
Salt and freshly ground black pepper
1 cup diced tomatoes
3 tablespoons thinly sliced fresh basil plus 8 basil leaves for garnish
2 tablespoons unsalted butter
⅓ cup freshly grated parmesan

Put ¼ cup of the olive oil in a heavy saucepan over medium-high heat. Sauté the onion and garlic for 2 minutes, stirring continuously. Add the curry and ground chilies and continue to stir with a wooden spoon for about 2 minutes. Add the rice, stirring to coat with the oil, spices, and onion.

Add the wine and cook, stirring frequently, until the liquid is absorbed, about 3 minutes. Add 2 cups of the stock and stir frequently while the rice simmers.

Meanwhile, put the remaining ¼ cup oil in a medium skillet over high heat. Add the squid and scallops and cook for 1 minute. Add the shrimp and cook for 2 minutes. Season with salt and pepper to taste. Set aside.

Continue adding stock, 1 cup at a time, as each preceding cup is absorbed. After a total of 7 cups has been added, stir in the shellfish. Add the last cup of warm stock, if needed, and continue stirring until the rice has a creamy but not runny texture and the grains are plump and tender but somewhat firm. Cooking time from the first addition of stock is 23 to 26 minutes.

Stir in the tomatoes, basil, butter, and parmesan until the cheese is completely dissolved. Season with salt and pepper. Spoon into individual bowls and garnish with basil leaves.

spicy shrimp paella with clams and fava beans

serves 4

1 pound fava beans, shelled (1 cup)
Salt
¼ cup olive oil
1 pound medium-large shrimp (16 to 20), shelled and deveined with tails left on
2 cloves garlic, minced
¼ pound crumbled chorizo sausage or other spicy pork sausage
1 fresh chili pepper such as jalapeño, seeded and minced
2 ripe large tomatoes, peeled, seeded, and chopped (see page 17)
1 tablespoon saffron threads
3 quarts warm Shellfish or Chicken Stock (pages 16 and 15)
3 cups Spanish paella rice or other short-grain rice
36 Manila clams or other very small clams such as littlenecks, scrubbed
½ pound fresh peas, shelled (½ cup)
Freshly ground black pepper

Cook fava beans in 1 quart boiling salted water for 5 minutes or until just tender. Drain and run under cool water. When cooled, peel each bean by tearing off a small piece of the peel from the rounded end with your fingernail. Squirt the bean out by pinching the opposite end. Set aside.

Put the olive oil in a large paella pan or deep 14-inch skillet over medium-high heat. Add the shrimp and sauté for 1 minute per side. Remove and set aside.

Reduce heat to medium and sauté the garlic, chorizo, and chili pepper for 1 minute. Add the tomatoes and saffron and cook for 2 minutes. Add the warm stock and ½ teaspoon salt. Bring to a boil, reduce to a simmer, and cook, uncovered, for 45 minutes.

Add the rice and clams and stir well. Increase heat to high and bring to a boil. Reduce to medium-high and cook for 10 minutes without stirring. The rice should begin to swell. Stir in the fava beans and peas, ½ teaspoon salt, and ½ teaspoon pepper.

Place the shrimp in a circular pattern on top of the rice and cook, uncovered, over medium-low heat for 10 minutes, or until the liquid is almost completely absorbed. Remove the pan from the heat and allow to rest at room temperature, covered, for 10 minutes before serving. Serve in a shallow bowl or large platter with shrimp scattered on top.

In Spain, paella is traditionally cooked over an open fire, often in pans as big as wading pools. This version is designed for the stove in a more common household skillet, albeit a good-size one. My paella is also creamier than the classic paella and has fresh fava beans instead of the more common dried white beans. Serve it with a fruity, young—but not tannic—red wine from Spain or Italy.

basmati rice with eggplant, almonds, and basil

serves 6

Although basmati is native to India and more common there, it's a natural for the healthful dishes of the Mediterranean Rim, particularly the pilafs so common in the eastern Mediterranean. Fragrant and flavorful, basmati is great plain, but it also lends itself to seasoning with nuts, herbs, and spices while still retaining its natural flavor.

2 tablespoons sesame seeds
¼ cup sliced almonds
1 medium eggplant
3 tablespoons unsalted butter
1 tablespoon cumin seeds
1 shallot, chopped
1 teaspoon honey
2 cups basmati rice
10 basil leaves, stacked, rolled like a cigar, and cut crosswise into thin strips
Salt and freshly ground black pepper

Preheat the oven to 350 degrees. Put the sesame seeds on a small sheet pan or pie plate and toast for 6 minutes. Add almonds and toast for 8 to 9 minutes more, or until both are golden brown. Set aside.

Cut 1 inch off the top of the eggplant and discard. Peel and dice the eggplant into ¼-inch cubes.

Put 2 tablespoons of the butter in a large heavy-bottomed saucepan over medium-high heat. Add the cumin seeds, shallots, and eggplant and cook, stirring frequently with a wooden spoon, for 6 minutes. Add the almonds and sesame seeds and cook for 1 minute. Add the honey and raise the heat to high.

Add 4 cups of water and bring to a boil. Add the rice, stir, and cover. Reduce the heat to medium-low and simmer for 20 minutes. Stir in the remaining butter and the basil and season with salt and pepper to taste.

Serve as a side dish with Crisp Red Snapper with Onion Agrodolce (page 72) or another fish dish, or with lamb.

basmati pancake with saffron, honey, and mint

serves 4

1 ½ cups basmati rice
Salt
1 teaspoon ground cumin
½ teaspoon saffron threads dissolved in 2 teaspoons warm water
1 ½ tablespoons honey
Freshly ground black pepper
Olive oil spray
8 mint leaves, coarsely chopped

Preheat the oven to 450 degrees.

In a large saucepan, bring 3 cups of water to a boil. Add the rice and 1 teaspoon of salt. Cook, uncovered, for 12 minutes. Transfer rice to a strainer for about 5 minutes to drain out any moisture.

In a mixing bowl, blend the rice with the cumin, saffron water, and honey. Season with salt and pepper to taste.

Coat a 9-inch tart pan with a removable bottom with olive oil spray. Pack the rice evenly into the pan. Spray the top with more oil.

Bake for 14 to 15 minutes or until golden brown on top. Remove the sides of the pan and cut the pancake into 4 wedges. Serve with mint sprinkled on top.

I got the idea for this dish while thumbing through an Indian cookbook, looking for a side dish to go with a tuna entree that had a sauce. I wanted something crisp but not fried because I wanted to keep the amount of fat to a minimum. Besides being a fine side dish, the pancake could be a more substantial part of a meal with vegetables and condiments such as Romesco (page 152) or Mint Chutney (page 155).

cavatelli with grilled vegetables and sheep's milk feta

serves 4

Most available feta is mass-produced from cow's milk and has a sharp edge to it. Sheep's milk feta is much creamier and more mild, but it still contains a rich feta flavor. It also melts better, making it ideal for pizzas and pastas like this one.

6 ripe plum tomatoes, cut lengthwise
½ cup plus 2 tablespoons extra virgin olive oil
Salt and freshly ground black pepper
1 tablespoon balsamic vinegar
Leaves from 2 sprigs fresh thyme, chopped
Needles from 2 sprigs fresh rosemary, chopped
½ small bulb fennel
1 medium zucchini, ends trimmed and quartered lengthwise
1 clove garlic, chopped
4 tablespoons very coarsely chopped kalamata olives
½ cup Chicken Stock (page 15)
2 tablespoons unsalted butter
1 pound cavatelli, radiatori (shown) or any short pasta such as penne, rigatoni, or fusilli, cooked according to package directions
2 tablespoons chopped parsley
½ cup sheep's milk feta, crumbled

Preheat the oven to 200 degrees. Sprinkle the tomatoes with 2 tablespoons of the olive oil, and season with salt and pepper to taste. Place, cut side up, on a baking sheet and bake until partially dried but still retaining some moisture, about 1 hour and 40 minutes. Cut crosswise into ½-inch-wide slices and set aside.

Set up a charcoal or gas grill at high heat with the grate about 4 inches from the heat source. In a medium bowl, combine ¼ cup of the remaining oil, vinegar, thyme, half of the rosemary, and salt and pepper to taste. Remove and discard the green stalks from the fennel and cut out and discard the hard inner core. Cut lengthwise into 6 to 8 wedges. Toss the fennel and zucchini in the marinade. Grill the zucchini for about 4 minutes and the fennel for 5 to 6 minutes, or until both are tender. Cut both crosswise into ½-inch pieces.

Put the remaining ¼ cup oil in a large skillet over medium heat. Add the garlic and the remaining rosemary and sauté for 1 minute. Add the zucchini, fennel, olives, and tomatoes and sauté for 1 minute. Add the stock and reduce the liquid by half, about 2 minutes. Add the butter and cook until melted. Add the cavatelli, parsley, and feta. Stir to coat the pasta. Adjust the salt and pepper and serve.

toasted barley risotto with wild mushrooms

serves 4 as a main course
or 6 as an appetizer

Barley is perhaps the oldest cultivated grain in the Mediterranean, going back some seven thousand years in Egypt. It was the primary grain in Europe before it was supplanted by wheat. When cooked slowly in the style of a risotto, barley becomes rich and creamy while retaining its natural texture. Barley's earthy flavor goes well with fall and winter ingredients like the wild mushrooms in this dish, and also with chestnuts and winter squash.

¼ cup hazelnuts
2 cups pearl barley
2 tablespoons olive oil
1 clove garlic, chopped
2 tablespoons minced shallots
2 cups assorted wild mushrooms such as portobello, oyster, shiitake, and porcini, chopped
½ cup dry white wine
5 cups warm Chicken Stock (page 15)
2 tablespoons unsalted butter
1 tablespoon honey
1 teaspoon ground cardamom
1 cup grated parmesan
Salt and freshly ground black pepper
2 tablespoons chopped chives

Preheat the oven to 350 degrees. Put the hazelnuts on a small sheet pan or pie plate and toast for 11 minutes, or until browned but not dark. Wrap the nuts in a clean dish towel and rub off skins. Chop and set aside.

Put a large nonstick skillet over low to medium heat. Add the barley and gently toss for 4 minutes. Put the oil in a large heavy-bottomed saucepan over medium heat, add the garlic and shallots, and sauté for 2 to 3 minutes, or until shallots soften but garlic does not get too dark. Add the mushrooms and cook for 2 to 3 minutes. Add the barley and stir until coated with oil.

Add the white wine and allow it to evaporate, about 1 minute. Add 2 cups of the stock. Continue adding stock, 1 cup at a time, as soon as each previous cup is absorbed, until the barley is firm but cooked, 20 to 25 minutes from the first addition of stock. Add the hazelnuts with the last cup of stock. Stir in the butter, honey, cardamom, and ½ cup of the parmesan. Season with salt and pepper to taste.

Serve in individual shallow bowls or soup plates, garnished with the remaining parmesan and chives.

bulgur with fava beans

serves 8

1 ⅓ cups bulgur (about ½ pound)
4 cups boiling water
½ cup pine nuts (about 3 ounces)
2 pounds fava beans, shelled (about 2 cups), or 2 cups frozen baby lima beans, thawed
½ cup seeded and finely diced tomato
2 cloves garlic, minced
½ cup chopped dates
½ cup fresh lemon juice
½ cup olive oil
Salt and freshly ground black pepper
2 tablespoons finely chopped cilantro

Put the bulgur in large mixing bowl and pour the boiling water over. Stir and let stand, uncovered, until the bulgur is soft and chewy, about 30 minutes.

Meanwhile, preheat the oven to 350 degrees. Put the pine nuts on a small sheet pan or pie plate and toast for 9 to 10 minutes, or until golden brown. Set aside.

Cook the fava beans in 1 quart of boiling salted water for 5 minutes, or until just tender. Drain and run under cool water. When cooled, peel each bean from its shell by tearing off a small piece of peel from the rounded end with your fingernail. Squirt out the bean out by pinching the opposite end. Set beans aside. (If using limas, blanch them in boiling water until tender, about 2 minutes.)

Drain the bulgur in a fine sieve, pressing lightly to extract as much water as possible. Return to the mixing bowl and stir in the fava beans, tomato, garlic, dates, lemon juice, and oil. Season with salt and pepper to taste. Let stand at room temperature for 1 to 3 hours to allow the flavors to blend. Stir in the cilantro and pine nuts.

Despite its satisfying whole-grain flavor, bulgur doesn't have the following in America that rice or couscous do. But in eastern Mediterranean countries, it is quite common. In Turkey, bulgur (a Turkish word) is often used instead of rice in pilafs. This dish is a good choice for picnics because it travels well and won't spoil easily. If prepared far in advance, it may become a bit dry, in need of a little more oil and lemon and perhaps a touch of salt. Other grains such as rice, barley, or couscous can be used in this recipe, and other nuts and dried fruits may be substituted.

couscous with chicken, almonds, and squash

serves 4

In Morocco, couscous is steamed in a couscoussière, a two-part pot with a perforated top, but a number of makeshift couscous steamers are possible. The easiest, which I use, is a colander lined with cheesecloth. Other choices include metal or wooden vegetable steamers lined with cheesecloth or a large fine mesh sieve. The primary consideraton is that the holes be small enough to prevent the couscous from falling through.

1 ½ cups sliced almonds
¼ cup olive oil
1 chicken (3 pounds), cut into 8 serving pieces
2 medium onions, diced
2 pounds butternut squash, peeled, seeded, and cut into ½-inch cubes (about 3 ½ cups)
1 tablespoon turmeric
Pinch of saffron
1 tablespoon cinnamon
½ cup canned chick peas, rinsed and drained
8 cups Chicken Stock (page 15)
4 cups instant couscous (about 1 ½ pounds)
¼ cup chopped cilantro
Salt and freshly ground black pepper

Preheat the oven to 350 degrees. Put the almonds on a small sheet pan or pie plate and toast for 8 to 9 minutes, or until browned but not too dark. Set aside.

Put 2 tablespoons of the olive oil in a Dutch oven over medium-high heat. Add the chicken and cook until lightly browned, 6 to 7 minutes. Work in batches to avoid crowding the pan, which will make it harder to brown the chicken. Remove the chicken to a platter. Add the onions and squash and cook for 5 to 6 minutes, or until the onions soften. Return the chicken to the pot and add the turmeric, saffron, and cinnamon. Cook for 2 minutes, stirring well.

Add the chick peas and stock and bring to a boil over high heat. Reduce the heat to a simmer and cook for about 30 minutes, uncovered, or until the chicken is tender and the squash is cooked. Season with salt and pepper.

Put the couscous in a steamer lined with cheesecloth and place over the simmering stew. Cover and cook for 16 minutes, or until the couscous is cooked and looks swollen. Transfer the couscous to a decorative shallow bowl and season with ½ cup of the stew liquid, the remaining olive oil, and salt and pepper to taste.

Add the almonds and cilantro to the stew. Check the seasoning again, place the chicken pieces and vegetables in the middle of the couscous, and pour the broth around the edges. Serve immediately.

seafood

One of the biggest differences between cooking in America and the cooking of the Mediterranean Rim is how seafood is prepared. There is a great variety of fish to work with and it is usually cooked in a very simple and natural fashion. I grew up in Maine eating the freshest seafood imaginable—lobsters and crabs consumed within an hour or two after the fishing boats docked. I took freshness for granted, but I didn't realize how important simplicity is for seafood until I traveled to the Mediterranean.

At a tiny seafood restaurant in Portofino, Italy, I had the best scampi of my life. They were so fresh and so carefully grilled that the flesh of the shrimp had a creamy quality. They were adorned with nothing more than good olive oil, sea salt, freshly cracked pepper, and lemon. Not long afterwards, I had a similar preparation in New York, but it wasn't as good. The oil and seasonings were less than top quality, and the shrimp wasn't as fresh or as lovingly cooked. Message: You can't hide inferior ingredients when you cook seafood.

Pan-Roasted Cod with Provençal Fava Bean Ragout

Your first obligation when cooking seafood is to buy the freshest you can find, regardless of what kind it is. If sea bass looks best that day, buy it and adjust your meal plans accordingly. Don't blindly buy salmon just because that's what you had in mind.

The second duty is to fit the cooking to the seafood. There is a misconception that all chefs want their fish cooked rare in the middle. On the contrary, I believe that white-fleshed fish, like sea bass, should be cooked through until translucent but not flaky. Properly cooked, such fish should have a springy texture when pressed with a finger. Salmon and tuna, on the other hand, can be rare in the middle, like a good steak. Swordfish falls somewhere in between.

While simplicity is the order of the day in many seafood preparations, some fruits of the sea can tolerate heavier and more complex preparations like my Moroccan Spiced Crab Cakes. These dishes tend to involve fish and shellfish with a richness that isn't easily overpowered—scallops, crab, lobster (Grilled Lobster with Tomato-Coriander Dressing, for instance), tuna, salmon, herring, sardines, anchovies, monkfish, bluefish, mackerel, even cod when it is cut into thick steaks, as for Pan-Roasted Cod with Provençal Fava Bean Ragout.

When combining more than one kind of seafood, try to achieve harmony by putting together ingredients that have similar textures and flavors. For example, an oily fish like tuna would be inappropriate with scallops. But scallops go extremely well with other shellfish, like clams and shrimp, which is why this book contains several shellfish combinations such as Curried Shellfish Risotto (page 56) and Spicy Shrimp Paella with Clams and Fava Beans (page 57). Shellfish are also outstanding together in stews like the Spanish zarzuela.

Sometimes a contrast can give a dish that boost of flavor you're looking for. For example, the Portuguese and Spanish are fond of adding pork to fish, particularly shellfish. In that vein, my paella has chorizo, the spicy Spanish sausage.

Because I'm a texture fanatic, I like to give fish fillets texture with crusts made from nuts and ground seasonings, as in my Tuna with Almond-Sesame Crust. The crust adds flavor and crunchiness to the outside of the fish—and it seals in moisture.

To achieve every ounce of flavor I can (and to save a few pennies), I always use the cleaned bones and heads of fish and the shells of shellfish to make flavorful stocks. I urge you to do the same. (You will find a recipe for Shellfish Stock on page 16, which can be adapted for a fish stock by substituting fish bones or heads for the shrimp shells.) Just make sure to call ahead and ask your fishmonger to save these items for you because they're often gone by midday. Even if you have to pay a small amount for them, it's worth it.

At that Portofino restaurant, I also had a great seafood risotto, but with no seafood! Instead, it had the essence of seafood concentrated in a superb stock. As a result, it was better than most seafood risottos I've eaten that were chock-full of fish and shellfish.

serves 4

pan-roasted cod with provençal fava bean ragout

The old definition of a ragout was a French meat stew, with the flavors melding together after long, slow cooking. But to me, a ragout is a combination of ingredients in which each one retains its flavor while at the same time producing a superior finished product. Such is the result achieved with fava beans, ripe summer tomatoes, garlic, and olives in this dish, which comes together much more quickly than a traditional ragout. Liberal substitutions can be made, such as green olives or caperberries for the kalamata olives, other fresh shell beans for the favas, and halibut, grouper, or other firm-flesh white fish for cod.

⅓ cup coarse bread crumbs
2 tablespoons coarsely cracked coriander seeds
4 cod steaks or fillets (6 ounces each)
Salt
8 ounces fava beans, shelled (about ½ cup)
5 tablespoons olive oil
2 cloves garlic, minced
1 small tomato, diced
⅓ cup kalamata olives, pitted
4 teaspoons small capers, drained
¼ cup dry white wine
½ cup Shellfish or Chicken Stock (pages 16 and 15)
12 basil leaves, stacked, rolled like a cigar, and cut crosswise into thin strips
Freshly ground black pepper

Mix the bread crumbs with the coriander seeds and spread on a large plate. Press one side of the steaks firmly into the bread crumb mixture to coat well. Refrigerate up to 1 hour, if desired.

Cook the shelled fava beans in 1 quart of boiling salted water for 3 minutes. Drain and run under cool water. When cooled, peel skins by tearing off a small piece of peel from the rounded end with your fingernail. Squirt out the beans by pinching the opposite end. Set aside.

Preheat the oven to 200 degrees. Heat 4 tablespoons of the olive oil in a large nonstick skillet over medium-high heat. Add the fish, crust side down, and cook for about 3 minutes, or until the coating turns golden brown. Turn the fish over and cook for 5 to 6 minutes, or until the fish is springy to the touch and cooked through. Remove the fish to an ovenproof platter, cover loosely with foil, and put into the oven.

Wipe out the skillet with a paper towel and heat the remaining tablespoon of olive oil over high heat. Add the garlic and tomato and cook for 2 minutes. Reduce the heat to medium, add the fava beans, olives, and capers and cook for 1 minute. Add the wine and stock and turn the heat to high. Reduce the liquid by half, about 5 minutes. Remove from the heat, stir in the basil, and season with salt and pepper to taste.

Divide the fish among 4 plates and spoon the sauce evenly over and around the fish. Serve immediately.

tunisian-style sea bass with chili and saffron

serves 4

2 red bell peppers
8 plum tomatoes, peeled (see page 17)
5 tablespoons chopped cilantro
2 cloves garlic, chopped
½ teaspoon ground cumin
½ teaspoon ground dried chilies such as ancho, or chili powder
¼ teaspoon saffron threads
1 teaspoon paprika
Pinch of salt
Pinch of freshly ground black pepper
Pinch of cayenne
¼ cup Spicy Olive Oil (page 13)
4 Chilean or striped sea bass fillets (5 to 6 ounces each)
½ cup Shellfish Stock (page 16)
1 can (8 ounces) chick peas, rinsed and drained

Preheat the broiler. Put the peppers on a sheet pan lined with foil and broil for about 15 minutes, turning once or twice to ensure they blister and blacken evenly. Remove to a bowl, cover with plastic wrap, and let cool. Peel, seed, and cut into ½-inch-wide strips. Set aside. Cut the tomatoes lengthwise into eighths. Set aside.

Preheat the oven to 350 degrees.

In a small bowl, combine 2 tablespoons of the cilantro, the garlic, cumin, chilies, saffron, paprika, salt, black pepper, cayenne, and olive oil. Rub each fillet with 1 teaspoon of this mixture and add the remainder to the stock. Warm the stock in a small saucepan.

Place the fish tightly in a baking dish. Spread the chick peas, tomatoes, and peppers evenly on top of the fish. Pour the stock over and cover with foil. Bake for 15 minutes, remove the foil, and bake 5 minutes more. Transfer the fish to a platter, surround with the vegetables and pour cooking liquid over. Sprinkle with the remaining cilantro.

Serve with couscous.

The key to this dish is simplicity. It is baked in—and can be served from—one pan. The chili spice seasoning is very reminiscent of Tunisian cooking but there is no need to make a separate chili paste like harissa, which the Tunisians use in almost everything.

crisp red snapper with onion agrodolce

serves 4

Rice flour is becoming more and more available with the rapid increase of Asian markets throughout the country. Look for Chinese rice flour (made from long grain rice) rather than Japanese rice flour, which is made from glutinous rice. Pomegranate juice is available at Middle Eastern markets or by mail (see page 161). The interplay of sweet and sour—*agrodolce* in Italian—is very common in the Mediterranean, particularly with seafood.

1 large orange
2 tablespoons olive oil
2 large sweet onions such as Vidalia, chopped (about 3 cups)
¼ cup pine nuts
1 tablespoon sugar
2 tablespoons balsamic vinegar
Salt and freshly ground black pepper
2 tablespoons chopped chives
1 ½ cups pomegranate juice
1 teaspoon honey
1 teaspoon coarsely cracked coriander seeds
2 tablespoons fresh lemon juice
3 tablespoons unsalted butter
1 teaspoon chopped cilantro
Cayenne
½ cup rice flour
2 tablespoons baking powder
4 red snapper fillets (5 to 6 ounces each), skin on
¼ cup canola oil
24 steamed new potatoes
1 tablespoon chopped parsley

With a vegetable peeler, peel off four 2 x 1-inch strips from the orange. Blanch the strips in 2 cups boiling water for 2 minutes. Drain and cut into thin julienne strips. Juice the orange.

Put the olive oil in a heavy skillet over medium heat and cook the onions, covered, until translucent, about 5 minutes. Add the orange strips, pine nuts, and sugar. Raise the heat and add the orange juice and vinegar. Cook for 2 to 3 minutes, or until most of the liquid has evaporated. Season with salt and pepper to taste. Add the chives and set aside.

Combine the pomegranate juice, honey, coriander seeds, and lemon juice in a medium saucepan. Reduce to ¼ cup over medium-high heat, 14 to 16 minutes. Remove from the heat, stir in 1 tablespoon of the butter, the cilantro, and cayenne to taste. Taste for salt. Keep warm.

Preheat the oven to 400 degrees. In a shallow bowl, mix the rice flour, baking powder, ½ teaspoon salt, and 1 tablespoon cayenne with ½ cup water. Put the canola oil in a heavy ovenproof, nonstick skillet over medium-high heat. Dip the fish in the rice flour batter and cook, skin side up, for 2 to 3 minutes, turn and cook 2 to 3 minutes more until golden brown. Put into the oven for 3 minutes.

Toss the potatoes with the remaining 2 tablespoons butter and parsley and season with salt and pepper. Divide equally among 4 plates. Top with fish. Place the onion mixture to the side and drizzle with pomegranate sauce.

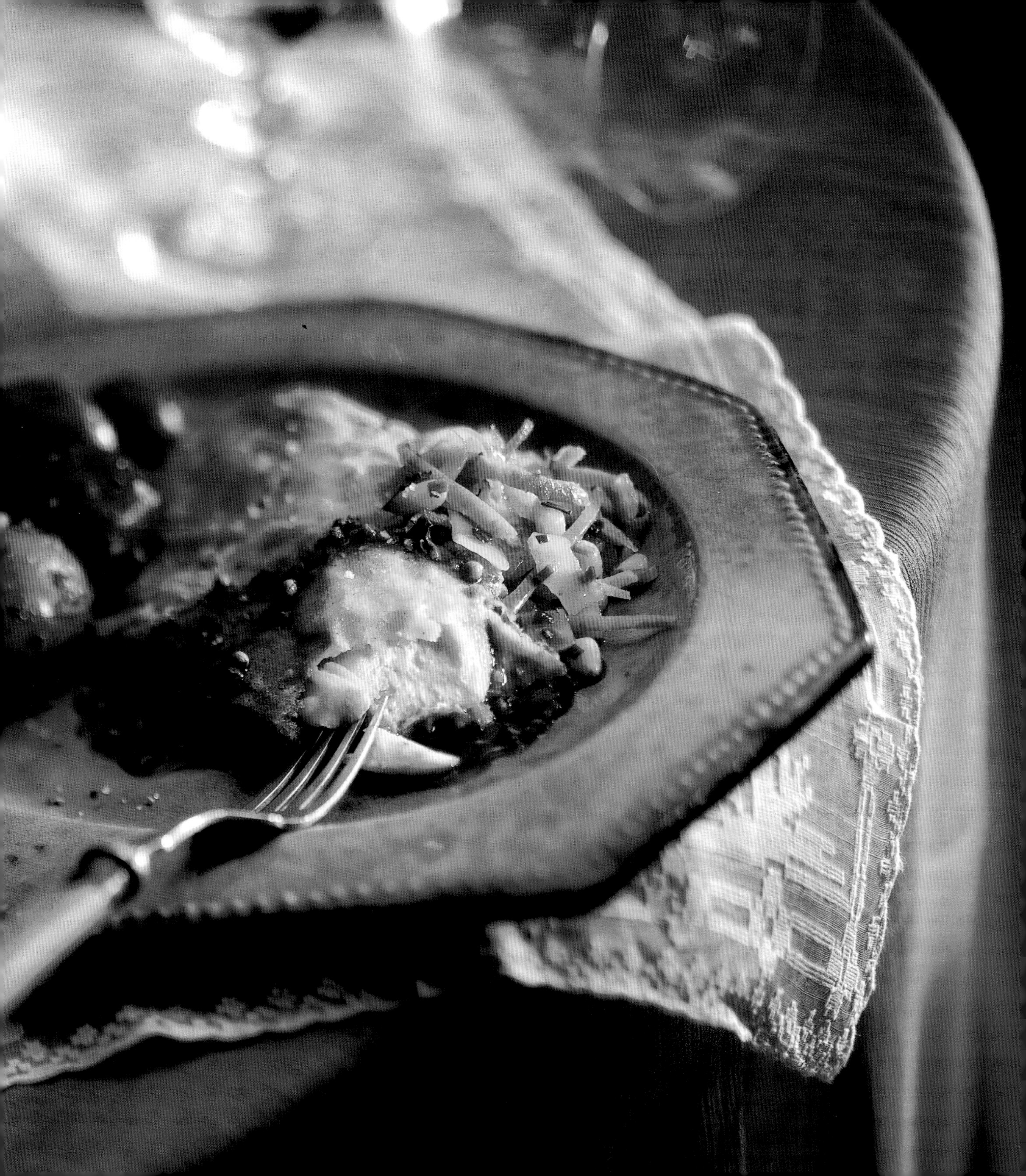

tuna tartar with fennel, caraway toast, and tapenade

serves 4 as a light luncheon entree or dinner first course

1 teaspoon caraway seeds
1 small bulb of fennel with leafy tops attached
2 tablespoons fresh lemon juice
2 teaspoons sherry vinegar
2 teaspoons minced shallots
3 to 4 tablespoons walnut oil
Kosher salt and freshly ground black pepper
8 ounces very fresh sashimi-grade tuna
1 teaspoon grated lemon zest
1 tablespoon olive oil
1 teaspoon light soy sauce
5 tablespoons chopped chives
Tabasco
2 tablespoons softened unsalted butter
4 slices brioche or other firm slicing bread or a crisp flatbread like lavash
½ cup Green Olive Tapenade (page 156)
2 tablespoons pitted and sliced picholine or other small green olives for garnish
1 teaspoon coarsely cracked black pepper

Put the caraway seeds in a heavy skillet over medium heat. Toast for 4 minutes, stirring a few times. Grind with a mortar and pestle or in a spice grinder. Set aside.

Wash the fennel and remove green stalks and leafy green tops. Discard the stalks and set leafy tops aside. Cut the bulb lengthwise in half and remove the hard center core from each half. With the flat side on a cutting board, cut each half in half again, horizontally. Then slice lengthwise into strips. Then cut crosswise into ⅛- to ¼-inch dice. In a mixing bowl, combine 2 tablespoons of the lemon juice, the vinegar, shallots, and walnut oil. Season with salt and pepper to taste. Add the fennel to this mixture, toss, and set aside.

Preheat the broiler or outdoor grill.

Cut the tuna into ⅛-inch dice with a very sharp knife. Using a spoon, mix the diced tuna with the lemon zest, olive oil, soy sauce, and 3 tablespoons of the chives. Add a dash of Tabasco to taste and season with salt and pepper.

Mix the butter and caraway seeds, and a pinch of salt. Spread on the brioche and grill or broil until toasted medium brown, about 1 ½ minutes per side. Cut each slice into quarters.

Divide the fennel salad equally among 4 plates. Top with the seasoned tuna. Drizzle a heaping tablespoon of the tapenade over the fish, extending the drizzle onto the plate itself. Put the toast around the tuna, overlapping the quarters. Garnish with the olives, pepper, chives, and fennel.

This is a great example of a dish that probably doesn't exist anywhere along the Mediterranean Rim but that showcases some of the region's most prominent flavors. Tuna is one of the Mediterranean's most important fish. Wild fennel, which is more pungent than bulb fennel, grows all over the place. And olives are used in numerous dishes. To facilitate cutting the tuna, make sure you have a very sharp knife and either rub it on a lightly oiled towel periodically or spray it with olive oil cooking spray.

serves 4

tuna with almond-sesame crust

The combination of fish, tomato, and almonds is very Catalonian. This dish would have an all-almond crust if the almonds stuck to the fish as easily as the sesame seeds, but they don't. So I've used the sesame seeds as a kind of binder to help the almonds adhere. Care is needed to avoid burning the crust during cooking. There's no magic to that other than to use a heavy-bottomed skillet and to be very watchful.

¼ cup blanched almonds
¼ cup sesame seeds
1 teaspoon sea salt
½ teaspoon freshly black ground pepper
¼ cup olive oil
4 tuna steaks, about 4 to 5 x 1¼ inches (6 ounces each)
½ cup Tomato Jam (page 153)
2 tablespoons chopped cilantro

Preheat the oven to 350 degrees. Put the almonds on a small sheet pan or pie plate and toast for 2 to 3 minutes. Add the sesame seeds and toast for 14 to 15 minutes longer, or until the almonds are browned but not too dark and the sesame seeds are golden brown. Finely chop the almonds and sesame seeds together. Keep the oven on.

Mix the sesame seeds, almonds, salt and pepper together on a plate. On another plate, coat the tuna steaks with 2 tablespoons of the olive oil. Roll the tuna steaks in the sesame-almond mixture, evenly coating each side of the fish.

Put the remaining 2 tablespoons oil in a large nonstick skillet over medium-high heat. Carefully sear the steaks in the skillet, about 1 minute per side, turning to brown each side and being mindful not to burn the crust mixture. Place the pan in the 350-degree oven and cook for 2 to 3 additional minutes, or until the fish is rare but warm in the middle. The edges of the fish will be quite firm but the middle will be springy.

Remove the fish from the pan and slice crosswise into ¼-inch-thick slices. Divide evenly among 4 plates, overlapping the slices. Top with the jam and cilantro.

A good accompaniment would be Spinach with White Raisins and Capers (page 126).

moroccan spiced crab cakes

serves 6

The Moroccan spice mixture that goes into these crab cakes is perfect with the rich crabmeat. Another unique element is the panko Japanese bread crumbs, which give the crab cakes a special crispness. If you are unable to find them at a local Asian grocery store, order by mail from the Katagiri Company (see page 161) or use fresh, very coarse bread crumbs from light bread. Almond flour may be difficult to get, though it is often available in health food stores. If you can't find it, just double the amount of bread crumbs.

1 ½ cups panko Japanese bread crumbs
1 ½ cups almond flour
2 tablespoons olive oil
1 small red bell pepper, seeded and finely chopped
2 ribs celery, finely chopped
2 tablespoons minced fresh ginger (about a 2-inch piece)
½ teaspoon chopped garlic
6 to 8 green onions, white parts only, thinly sliced
1 teaspoon ground cardamom
1 tablespoon ground cumin
1 tablespoon turmeric
1 cup heavy cream
1 pound jumbo lump crabmeat, picked through for shells
¼ cup chopped parsley
¼ cup chopped chives
2 tablespoons grated lemon zest
Pinch of cayenne
Salt
¼ cup canola oil
1 cup Cilantro Dressing (recipe follows)

Mix the panko with the almond flour. Set aside.

Put the olive oil in a large skillet over high heat and sauté the bell pepper and celery until the vegetables begin to soften, about 2 minutes. Reduce the heat to medium and add the ginger, garlic, and green onions. Stir and cook for 2 minutes. Add the cardamom, cumin, and turmeric and cook for 1 minute.

Add the cream, raise the heat to medium-high, and reduce by half, 6 to 7 minutes. Add the crabmeat and two thirds of the bread crumb mixture, half of the parsley, and half of the chives. Mix well and add the lemon zest, cayenne, and salt to taste. Let cool. Form into cakes with your hands, each about 3 inches in diameter and ½ inch thick. (You should have 12 to 14 cakes.) Dip the top and bottom lightly into the remaining bread crumbs. Refrigerate on a sheet pan lined with wax paper until ready to cook.

Put the canola oil into a skillet over medium-high heat. Add the crab cakes and fry 3 minutes on each side. Put 2 crab cakes each on 6 plates and drizzle with the Cilantro Dressing. Garnish with the remaining parsley and chives.

cilantro dressing

makes about 1 cup

1 cup fresh orange juice
2 teaspoons cumin seeds
1 cup cilantro leaves
½ cup canola oil
1 tablespoon fresh lemon juice
1 egg (see note)
Salt
Cayenne

Put the orange juice in a small saucepan over medium-high heat and reduce to ¼ cup, 12 to 14 minutes. Allow to cool.

Meanwhile, put the cumin seeds in a heavy skillet over medium heat. Toast for 4 minutes, stirring a few times. Grind with a mortar and pestle or in a spice mill.

Puree the orange juice with the cilantro in a blender or food processor until smooth. Add the oil, cumin, and lemon juice and mix well. Add the egg and mix well. Season with salt and cayenne to taste.

NOTE In recent years, some outbreaks of salmonella have been traced to raw eggs. If you are concerned about the safety of the eggs in your area, omit the egg from the dressing. The dressing will have a thinner consistency but the flavor will still be good.

grilled lobster with tomato-coriander dressing

serves 4

Though most people like their lobster straight, with perhaps some melted butter, I like to play with its flavor in different cooking methods. Grilling is a simple technique I often use with lobster and other crustaceans. Unlike fish or poultry, the flesh retains moisture because it is protected by a shell. Charcoal flavors act as a foil to the richness of the lobster meat. The tomato-coriander dressing could be from almost any country along the Mediterranean Rim.

Sea salt and freshly ground black pepper
4 lobsters (1 ½ pounds each)
1 tablespoon coriander seeds
¼ cup Spicy Olive Oil (page 13)
2 cloves garlic, minced
4 ripe medium tomatoes, peeled, seeded, and diced (see page 17)
1 cup dry white wine
¼ cup cilantro leaves, coarsely chopped
¼ cup olive oil

Heat a charcoal grill to medium-high or preheat the broiler.

In a large pot, bring 4 quarts of water and ¼ cup sea salt to a boil. Plunge the lobsters, one at a time, into the boiling water for 2 minutes. Remove and place on a cutting board. Crack the lobster claws with a nutcracker or mallet. Set aside.

Put the coriander seeds in a heavy skillet over medium heat, toast for 4 minutes, stirring a few times. Coarsely grind in a mortar and pestle or a spice grinder.

In a large saucepan, heat the Spicy Olive Oil over medium-high heat. Add the garlic and cook for 1 minute. Add the tomatoes and cook for 6 to 8 minutes, or until the juices begin to evaporate. Add the wine and ground coriander seeds and cook for about 10 minutes, or until the wine has completely evaporated. Remove from the heat, season with salt and pepper to taste, and add the cilantro. Let cool to room temperature.

Brush the lobsters with olive oil. Put on the charcoal grill close to the heat source but not touching the flame. Grill for 12 minutes, turning once. Or broil for 6 to 8 minutes, 6 to 8 inches from the heat source.

To serve, using a large heavy knife, cut the lobsters through the center of the head and tail. Remove and discard the tomalley (the green, liverlike organ). Leave the pink coral (eggs) intact or swirl them into the tomato sauce. Place the 2 lobster halves on large plates, with the meat side of the tails facing up and the claws facing outward. Spoon the tomato-coriander mixture over the lobster tails and serve any remaining sauce for dipping.

shrimp with lemon, garlic, and almonds

makes 4 servings

1 cup blanched almonds
2 cups Shellfish Stock (page 16)
½ teaspoon saffron threads, crushed
5 tablespoons extra virgin olive oil
1-inch-thick slice Italian bread, crust removed
4 cloves garlic, minced
¼ cup minced parsley
1 tablespoon minced lemon zest
½ teaspoon ground dried chilies such as ancho, or chili powder
1 pound medium-large shrimp (16 to 20), shelled and deveined with tails left on
3 tablespoons fresh lemon juice
Salt and freshly ground black pepper

Preheat the oven to 350 degrees. Put the almonds on a small sheet pan or pie plate and toast for 17 minutes, or until browned but not too dark. Set aside.

Meanwhile, bring the stock to a simmer, add the saffron and cook, uncovered, over medium heat for 8 to 10 minutes. Keep warm.

Put 2 tablespoons of the olive oil in a medium skillet over medium heat. Add the bread and cook about 1 minute on each side, or until medium dark brown. Remove and dry on paper towels. Break into 1-inch pieces.

Chop the almonds, garlic, 2 tablespoons of the parsley, the lemon zest, and bread in a food processor. Add 2 tablespoons of the stock and the ground chilies and blend to form a dry paste. Whisk the paste into the remaining stock. (The mixture should have some texture and not be smooth.)

Put the remaining olive oil in a medium-large over high heat. Add the shrimp and cook for 1 minute per side. Remove the shrimp and set aside. Add the stock mixture and lemon juice to the pan, reduce the heat to medium, and simmer for 8 minutes, or until thickened, with a chunky tomato texture. Add the shrimp and cook for 1 minute, or until the shrimp are cooked through but still tender. Season with salt and pepper to taste. To serve, transfer the shrimp to a terra cotta or other rustic serving bowl. Sprinkle with the remaining parsley.

Though my formal training is classical French, I prefer the textured sauces of the Mediterranean Rim to the strained, thinner sauces of haute cuisine. I like the way the former adhere to the other ingredients and become more integrated into the dish, rather than acting almost as a separate element. Here, the ground almonds carry flavors while coating the shrimp. Scallops, lobster, or almost any white-flesh fish can be substituted for the shrimp in this simple light stew with equally good results. Serve with a good crusty bread.

serves 4 as a main course

spicy shrimp frittata

Omelets, whether the Spanish tortilla (not to be confused with the Mexican bread) or the Italian frittata, are eaten at any time of the day in the Mediterranean. They can be served hot, warm, or at room temperature, for breakfast, lunch or dinner, as part of a mezze or antipasto table, or as a snack at a tapas bar. The basic elements of my frittata are eggs, green onions, and shallots. This framework can be filled in with any number of ingredients from shellfish to wild mushrooms, grilled vegetables or sausages, or a combination of all these.

3 tablespoons olive oil
4 green onions, white parts and all but top 1 inch of green parts, minced
1 clove garlic, minced
1 shallot, minced
¼ teaspoon ground dried chilies such as ancho, or chili powder
1 pound medium-large shrimp (16 to 20), shelled, deveined, and cut into ½-inch pieces
6 large eggs
2 tablespoons milk
½ teaspoon salt
¼ teaspoon freshly ground black pepper

Preheat the oven to 400 degrees.

Put the olive oil in a nonstick ovenproof skillet over medium-high heat. Add the green onions, garlic, shallot, ground chilies, and shrimp and sauté for 2½ minutes, or until the shrimp become opaque.

In a medium bowl, beat the eggs with the milk, salt, and pepper. Add them to the skillet, stirring with a wooden spoon. When the bottom of the frittata begins to set, after a few minutes, place the skillet in the oven. Bake for 10 minutes, or until firm to the touch.

Remove the skillet from the oven. Invert the frittata onto a plate, then flip back, right side up, onto another plate.

Serve with Almond-Caper Potato Salad (page 45) or a green salad.

poultry and game birds

Poultry and game birds are a natural fit for Mediterranean Rim cooking. Their lean and light texture is a perfect complement to the fresh herbs, olives, and capers of southern Italy, the powerful spices of the eastern Mediterranean, and the tomatoes and summer produce of France. And they lend themselves to one of my favorite cooking methods, something I call "crisping and glazing." Most of the poultry I prepare is cooked to crackling crisp on the stove or in the oven, then glazed with a sauce that often contains dried fruit or honey.

The other thing I like about poultry and game birds is their flexibility. A preparation for duck can often be transferred to squab or guinea hen with similar results. Chicken, however, may be overpowered by some seasoning used for game birds. With all poultry and game birds the skin and meat are tender and permeable, making them excellent candidates for marinades.

Moroccan Spiced Squab

Not all poultry and game birds can be cooked the same way, though. When deciding how to cook birds, I always consider size, the amount of fat, and the richness or color of the meat. If I had to choose just one of those qualities to determine my cooking method, it would be the amount of fat under the skin. For example, quail is very lean with a low percentage of fat. If it is cooked too slowly, the skin will not be crisp when the flesh is done. Therefore, quail is best seared on top of the stove to lock in moisture, then finished quickly in a hot oven.

Technique can also determine the type and amount of seasoning. Many spices become more intense with longer cooking times, while the flavor of fresh herbs tends to dissipate. In the end, the richness of the meat is the ultimate arbiter of how a particular poultry or game product is flavored. I like to cook with dried fruits, citrus, and honey. Rich meats like squab, duck, and quail handle these flavors well, but lighter poultry, like commercial chicken, might be overwhelmed by their intensity and sweetness. So, instead of the stronger red wine vinegar, I'd use lighter lemon juice with chicken, or raisins with chicken instead of dates as I do with duck in my Crisp Sicilian Duck with Olives, Dates, and Almonds.

While I like bold flavors, highly seasoned dishes must still have balance. When I began cooking at Malvasia, my first restaurant job in New York, I fell in love with the magical combination of duck, green olives, and dates. I had always liked duck and dates together, but in that dish the briny tartness of the olives perfectly offsets not only the intensely sweet dates but the rich duck as well.

In order to create authentic Mediterranean Rim flavors without lengthy preparation times, I often use marinades and reductions. The intense flavor of preserved lemons, which Moroccans love with poultry, is duplicated in my Lemon Chicken with Pine Nuts and Green Olives by first marinating the chicken in olive oil and lemon zest and then reducing fresh lemon juice in the sauce for just a few minutes. The result is a dish that is somewhat different from, though just as intense and flavorful as, the Moroccan original.

Grilling poultry and other meats on skewers is a common method of cooking in the eastern Mediterranean, Sicily, and parts of North Africa. Kabobs are a good way to entertain because they're festive—even if you don't carry them flaming through the dining room.

At one of the best summer parties I've attended in recent years, kabobs of chicken, lamb, and squid were served, each on different skewers, all cooked for different periods of time. They were laid out on a large platter on a picnic table along with several dipping sauces for guests to help themselves. You could do the same, starting with my Grilled Chicken Kabobs with Dipping Sauces. Add your own lamb, beef, or seafood kabobs and serve them with Tahini-Yogurt Sauce (page 158) or Middle Eastern Salsa Verde (page 151). For a very eastern Mediterranean touch, serve the kabobs with Flatbread (page 159).

Mediterraneans are not big on stuffing poultry, probably because traditional cooking methods involved spit-roasting poultry over an open fire instead of roasting in the oven. But poultry is ideal for stuffing because of its natural cavity. While I often make stuffing, I don't follow a precise formula and so I have not included a stuffing recipe in this book. However, here are some suggestions: I like grains such as cooked rice, barley, bulgur, or couscous. For added texture, I put in nuts or, if nuts aren't available, a crunchy vegetable like carrots or broccoli stems. And for a touch of sweetness I use dried fruit.

Though freshness in poultry and game isn't as important as it is with seafood, quality is. In many cases, poultry that is wrapped properly and kept frozen at sufficiently low temperatures is perfectly acceptable. If you buy fresh poultry but are not planning to cook it right away, I suggest you marinate it. Marinating will preserve the skin's moisture and add flavor as well. Chicken shouldn't marinate longer than twenty-four hours, but game birds, like the pheasant in Pheasant and Wild Mushrooms Roasted in Walnut Oil, will tolerate up to forty-eight hours of marinating.

If you can, buy free-range chickens or game birds, available at good meat markets and specialty food stores. You can taste the difference from mass-produced poultry. If local sources aren't possible, order by mail from companies like D'Artagnan (see page 161). With free-range chickens, it's wise to closely monitor cooking times because these birds are usually leaner and can easily overcook and dry out. The same, of course, is true of game.

spicy chicken breasts with tahini-yogurt sauce

serves 4

¼ cup olive oil
½ teaspoon hot paprika
½ teaspoon sweet paprika
½ teaspoon ground dried ancho chilies or chili powder
½ teaspoon ground cumin
4 chicken breast halves on the bone (8 to 11 ounces each), skin on
Salt and freshly ground black pepper
1 cup Tahini-Yogurt Sauce (page 158)

Preheat the oven to 425 degrees.

Mix 2 tablespoons of the olive oil and the spices in a small bowl. Put the chicken and spices in a mixing bowl and toss. Season with salt and pepper to taste. Put the remaining 2 tablespoons olive oil in an ovenproof skillet over medium heat.

Brown the chicken 1½ to 2 minutes on the meaty side, then turn and brown for 3 to 4 minutes on the skin side. Pour out any excess oil. Transfer the skillet to the oven and cook for about 30 minutes, or until the chicken is just cooked through. Serve with Tahini-Yogurt Sauce.

One of the major advantages of Mediterranean Rim cooking is that so much flavor can be derived quickly from marinades, spice mixtures, and easy sauces that don't require the preparation of a stock or base but can be made with basic pantry elements. This chicken dish is a perfect example. The coolness of the Tahini-Yogurt Sauce balances the spices perfectly. Serve this with a green salad.

lemon chicken with pine nuts and green olives

serves 4

The first time I tasted Moroccan lemon chicken I knew I wanted to create my own version as a signature dish. I loved the taste, but it was a bit heavy and the skin wasn't crisp the way I normally like it. So I lightened it somewhat while still retaining the intense flavor of the original and making the skin crisp. The result is a dish worth the high number of ingredients and twenty-four-hour marinating time. Serve with Spinach with White Raisins and Capers (page 126) and couscous or grilled flatbread.

½ cup olive oil
1 lemon, zest cut into julienne strips and juice reserved
Crushed red pepper
2 chickens (2 ½ pounds each)
¼ cup pine nuts
Salt and freshly ground black pepper
5 tablespoons grated onion
1 tablespoon minced garlic
1 tablespoon minced fresh ginger
Pinch of saffron
⅓ cup pitted and sliced Moroccan green olives or other green olives
2 tablespoons honey
2 cups Chicken Stock (page 15)
2 tablespoons unsalted butter
2 tablespoons chopped cilantro

Combine the olive oil, lemon zest, and a pinch of red pepper. Rub the chickens with the marinade, cover, and refrigerate for 6 to 24 hours.

Preheat the oven to 350 degrees. Put the pine nuts on small sheet pan or pie plate and toast for 9 to 10 minutes, or until golden brown. Set aside. Increase the oven temperature to 375 degrees.

Remove the chickens from the marinade, reserving the marinade, and season the chickens inside and out with salt and pepper. Truss the chickens. Heat a flameproof baking dish or roasting pan over high heat on top of the stove. Add 2 tablespoons of the olive oil from the marinade and brown the chickens until golden on both sides, 7 or 8 minutes. Place in the oven and roast for 35 to 40 minutes, or until the juices run pale yellow. Remove from the pan and set aside. Pour out all but 2 tablespoons of the fat.

On top of the stove over medium-high heat, add the onion, garlic, and ginger to the roasting pan. Cook until the onion just begins to brown, about 2 minutes. Add a pinch of red pepper, the pine nuts, saffron, olives, and lemon juice. Scrape the pan with a wooden spoon and let the liquid reduce slightly, 2 to 3 minutes. Add the honey and stock and reduce by half, about 6 to 7 minutes. Finish the sauce by swirling in the butter and adding the cilantro. Season with salt and pepper to taste. Keep warm.

Remove the trussing from the chickens and carve or quarter them. If more browning is desired, do so under the broiler. Spoon the sauce over the chicken and serve.

grilled chicken kabobs with dipping sauces

serves 4

Grilling pieces of meat and poultry on a skewer is one of the oldest cooking techniques, and one that is particularly popular in the lands around the Mediterranean. Try this dish for a change to your usual summer barbecue. Serve the kabobs with the sauces listed or simply with a squeeze of lemon and drizzle of olive oil.

1 teaspoon ground cumin
1 teaspoon ground ginger
1 teaspoon sweet paprika
¼ teaspoon cayenne
¼ cup olive oil
¼ cup fresh lemon juice
1 tablespoon honey
Salt
4 skinless and boneless chicken breast halves (about 6 ounces each), cut into 1-inch cubes
12 bamboo skewers (about 10 inches long)
1 medium red onion, peeled and cut into 8 equal sections
¼ cup chopped cilantro
1 cup Mint Chutney (page 155)
1 cup Hazelnut and Pomegranate Sauce (page 157)

In a large mixing bowl, combine the cumin, ginger, paprika, cayenne, olive oil, lemon juice, honey, and salt to taste. Toss the chicken cubes with the mixture, cover, and marinate for 2 hours.

While the chicken marinates, soak the skewers in water for 1 hour and prepare a charcoal grill to medium-high heat.

Separate the onion sections into leaves or triangular pieces. Alternate the chicken and onion pieces on skewers. You should have 4 or 5 pieces each of chicken and onion on each skewer.

Place the skewers about 4 inches from the heat, raising the grill rack if necessary to avoid burning. Grill, turning every 1½ minutes, until well browned and cooked through, 6 to 7 minutes. Or broil the kabobs 4 to 5 inches from the heat source for 6 to 7 minutes, turning every 1½ minutes.

Sprinkle with the cilantro and serve warm with Mint Chutney and Hazelnut and Pomegranate Sauces for dipping.

crisp sicilian duck with olives, dates, and almonds

serves 4

I was introduced to many taste sensations when I worked under Gennaro Picone, a very talented Italian chef from the island of Lipari near Sicily. One of his strengths was balancing sweet and sour flavors. This dish is a perfect example. The sweet and sour flavors are also a classic example of Sicilian cooking, so this dish will be featured on the menu at Monzù, my new Sicilian restaurant.

⅓ cup sliced almonds
2 Long Island ducks (3 pounds each), wing tips and excess fat removed
Salt and freshly ground black pepper
4 ribs celery, coarsely chopped
1 large onion, coarsely chopped
1 small bunch of fresh thyme, coarsely chopped
3 tablespoons olive oil
16 dried dates, pitted and sliced about ¼ inch thick
⅓ cup pitted and sliced (about ¼ inch thick) picholine or other small green olives
¼ cup sweet amber dessert wine such as muscat or vin santo
2 cups duck stock or Rich Chicken Stock (page 16)
¼ cup plus 2 tablespoons chopped parsley
2 tablespoons unsalted butter

Preheat the oven to 350 degrees. Put the almonds on a small sheet pan or pie plate and toast for 8 to 9 minutes, or until golden brown. Set aside. Increase oven temperature to 400 degrees.

Rub the ducks inside and out with salt and pepper. Combine the celery, onion, and thyme in mixing bowl. Stuff into the cavities of the ducks. Place the ducks on a rack in a roasting pan. Roast for about 1 hour, pouring off fat after 25 minutes and again after about 45 minutes. The skin should be crisp and golden brown. Remove from the oven, cover with foil, and keep warm.

Put the olive oil in a skillet over medium heat. Gently sauté the dates and olives until the dates begin to soften, about 3 minutes. Add the wine and reduce by half, 3 to 5 minutes. Add the almonds and stock and reduce by half, 8 to 10 minutes. Remove from the heat and stir in the ¼ cup parsley and butter. Season with salt and pepper.

Carve or quarter the ducks. Spoon the sauce over and sprinkle with the remaining parsley.

Serve with Tunisian Couscous Salad (page 39) or a baby spinach salad.

cornish hens with zucchini, sweet peppers, and za'atar

serves 4

The Lebanese believe za'atar (also spelled zahtar) gives strength and clears the mind. School children eat bread slathered with olive oil and za'atar before exams. Both a type of herb and an herb blend, Za'atar is available at Middle Eastern markets or spice shops or by mail from Kalustyan's (see page 161). But you can make your own (recipe follows). Za'atar can also be mixed with olive oil as a dip or to spread on grilled or roasted meat or fish or on grilled or toasted flatbread. Serve with Chopped Summer Salad with Feta, Favas, and Green Onions (page 40) and Olive Oil Mashed Potatoes (page 125).

2 red bell peppers
4 Cornish hens (about 1 pound each), split lengthwise in half
Salt and freshly ground black pepper, to taste
¼ cup Spicy Olive Oil (page 13)
4 tablespoons Za'atar (recipe follows)
8 cloves garlic, unpeeled
2 medium zucchini, trimmed and cut diagonally into ½-inch-thick slices
½ teaspoon crushed red pepper
1 tablespoon honey
1 tablespoon fresh lemon juice

Preheat the broiler. Put the peppers on a sheet pan lined with foil and broil for about 15 minutes, turning once or twice to ensure they blister and blacken evenly. Transfer to a bowl, cover with plastic wrap, and let cool. Peel, seed, and cut into ½-inch-wide strips. Set aside.

Preheat the oven to 400 degrees.

Season the hens inside and out with salt and pepper. Mix 2 tablespoons of the oil with 2 tablespoons of the Za'atar and rub the hens with this mixture. Put a roasting pan large enough to hold all the hens easily over high heat. (Use 2 pans if necessary.) Add the remaining oil and brown the hens, skin side down, until golden brown, about 6 minutes. Turn and add the garlic, zucchini, crushed red pepper and the roasted peppers. Toss well.

Transfer to the oven and roast for 18 to 20 minutes, uncovered, until just cooked through, tossing ingredients every 5 minutes. The juices should run pale pink.

Remove the hens and separate the legs from the breasts. Place the legs on 4 plates, skin side up, and lean the breasts against them, also skin side up. Toss the remaining ingredients with the honey and lemon juice. Taste for salt and pepper and adjust the seasoning if needed. Spread the vegetables and sauce evenly over the chicken. Garnish with the remaining 2 tablespoons Za'atar sprinkled on top.

za'atar

makes about 3/4 cup

½ cup dried thyme
¼ cup sumac
½ teaspoon sea salt
2 tablespoons toasted sesame seeds

NOTE: **Sumac is available by mail from Kalustyan's** **(see page 161).**

Preheat the oven to 350 degrees. Put the sesame seeds on a small sheet pan or pie plate and toast for 6 minutes.

Combine thyme, sumac, salt, and sesame seeds and grind into a fine powder in a spice mill. (This may require 2 batches.) Store in an airtight container for up to 3 to 4 months.

roasted quail with golden raisins and hazelnuts

serves 4

Italians are particularly fond of quail as it makes its migration from Sicily (where legend has it the birds saved the city of Siracuse from starvation) to the Marches to the Veneto (where it is often part of a risotto) to Piedmont (where it may be found atop polenta). Quail is remarkably compatible with a variety of ingredients, from fresh and dried fruits to cured meat like bacon and pancetta, to vinegar and wine. Whichever seasoning is used, the flavor of the meat comes through distinctly. Yet it's never overtly gamey. Since quail is often hunted in the fall, the hazelnuts in this recipe add a complementary seasonal touch.

¼ cup hazelnuts
2 heads Belgian endive
8 boneless quails
Salt and freshly ground black pepper
¼ cup olive oil
2 tablespoon fresh lemon juice
¼ cup Sauternes or other sweet white dessert wine
1 cup game stock or Rich Chicken Stock (page 16)
4 tablespoons golden (sultana) raisins
1 tablespoon unsalted butter
1 tablespoon chopped mint leaves

Preheat the oven to 350 degrees. Put the hazelnuts on a small sheet pan or pie plate and toast for 11 minutes, or until browned but not dark. Remove and cool slightly. Rub in a clean dish towel to remove the skins and coarsely chop. Set aside. Increase the oven temperature to 450 degrees.

Pull apart the leaves of the endive by cutting each head lengthwise in half and removing the firm core. The leaves will fall apart. Stack the leaves, a few at a time and cut lengthwise into thin strips. Set aside.

Rub the quails lightly inside out with salt and pepper. Put the olive oil in a roasting pan on top of the stove over high heat. Brown the quails, breast side down, for 2 to 2½ minutes. Brown the other side for the same length of time. Put the pan in the oven. Cook, breast side up, 8 to 10 minutes, or to medium-rare. The juices should run pale pink. Remove the quails from the pan and set on paper towels.

Pour out the oil from the pan and add the lemon juice and wine. Swirl the liquid and allow to settle about 30 seconds. Add the stock and put the pan over medium-high heat. Add the raisins and boil the liquid to reduce to one third of its volume, about 5 minutes. Remove the pan from the heat and add the butter, mint, and hazelnuts.

Spread the endive on a platter or individual plates and place the quails on top. Spoon the sauce over, distributing the raisins and hazelnuts evenly.

pheasant and wild mushrooms roasted in walnut oil

serves 4

Pheasant is a fall game bird that goes well with other autumn ingredients like wild mushrooms and nuts. While this preparation is very much in the Mediterranean style, which features strong marinades to tame gamey flavors, pheasant in the United States is usually milder because our birds are mostly domesticated. Care needs to be taken to avoid drying out the breast, which is why I cover it part of the time. You can also prepare quail, squab, or duck this way. Serve with Cardamom-baked Sweet Potatoes (page 127).

4 cups port wine
4 cloves garlic, chopped
1 tablespoon honey
2 sprigs of fresh thyme, leaves only, or ½ teaspoon dried thyme
2 pheasants (about 2 ½ pounds each)
½ cup walnuts
1 cup Rich Chicken stock (page 16)
6 tablespoons walnut oil
Salt and freshly ground black pepper
1 tablespoon unsalted butter
1 pound mixed wild mushrooms, such as shiitake, oyster, porcini, or portobello
2 tablespoons chopped parsley

Combine the port, garlic, honey, and thyme in a bowl just large enough to hold the pheasants. Place the pheasants in the marinade, cover, and refrigerate 24 to 48 hours.

Preheat the oven to 350 degrees. Put the walnuts on a small sheet pan or pie plate and toast for 13 minutes, or until they smell nutty and darken somewhat but are not dark. Set aside. Put the stock in a saucepan over medium-high heat and reduce by half, about 10 minutes. Set aside.

Remove the pheasants from the marinade, reserving the marinade, and pat dry with paper towels. Rub the pheasants generously with 4 tablespoons walnut oil and season with salt and pepper. Place on a shallow rack inside a roasting pan. Roast for 20 minutes, brushing the pheasants every 10 minutes with one-third of the marinade.

In a medium saucepan over medium-high heat, bring the stock and remaining marinade to a boil. Reduce to ½ cup, 20 to 25 minutes. Set aside.

Toss the mushrooms with the remaining walnut oil and season with salt and pepper. Put the mushrooms and walnuts around the pheasant. Cover the pheasant breasts with foil and cook for 25 minutes more (45 minutes total), removing the foil for the last 5 to 10 minutes to let the breast skin crisp. Remove the mushrooms, walnuts, and pheasants from the pan and let the pheasants sit 5 to 7 minutes, covered with foil.

Add the mushrooms and walnuts to the port sauce. Bring to a boil, reduce to a simmer, add the butter, and turn heat off. Season with salt and pepper.

To serve, halve the breasts and separate the legs. Arrange on 4 plates and evenly distribute the port sauce and mushrooms over the pheasant and sprinkle with parsley.

moroccan spiced squab

serves 4

1 teaspoon ground turmeric
1 teaspoon ground coriander
1 teaspoon ground ginger
1 teaspoon freshly ground black pepper
1 teaspoon ground cumin
4 squabs (1 to 1 ¼ pounds each)
¼ cup olive oil
4 teaspoons sesame seeds
Salt
⅔ cup coarsely chopped onion
⅔ cup coarsely chopped carrot
⅔ cup coarsely chopped celery
2 cloves garlic, chopped
Pinch of saffron threads
1 cup Chicken Stock (page 15)
2 tablespoons fresh lemon juice
1 tablespoon honey
3 tablespoons chopped cilantro
1 cup couscous, cooked according to package instructions
8 cilantro leaves, for garnish

Combine the turmeric, coriander, ginger, pepper, and cumin in a small bowl. Rub the squabs inside and out with 2 tablespoons of the olive oil, then with the spice mixture. Cover and refrigerate 2 hours.

Preheat the oven to 350 degrees. Put the sesame seeds on a small sheet pan or pie plate and toast for 14 to 15 minutes, or until golden brown. Set aside.

Increase the oven temperature to 400 degrees. Season the squabs with salt. Put the remaining 2 tablespoons oil in a large ovenproof skillet over medium-high heat. Brown the squabs on all sides, about 8 minutes, and set aside. Add the onion, carrot, celery, and garlic and sauté until the vegetables start to brown, about 5 minutes. Add the saffron and stir for 1 minute. Place the squabs on top of the vegetables. Mix together the stock, lemon juice, and honey, add to the skillet, and bring to a boil. Reduce to a simmer, cover tightly, and place in the oven until squabs are cooked through, about 15 minutes. The juices should run pink.

Remove the squabs and keep warm. Strain the sauce through a fine mesh strainer into a 1-quart saucepan and reduce over medium-high heat to two-thirds of its volume, about 6 minutes. Add the chopped cilantro.

Squab is rich and satisfying but not heavy. It also stands up to some of my favorite seasonings, the spices of Morocco. The cooking technique used in this recipe allows the sauce to absorb the flavor of both the spices and the squab. It's a complex taste that is often difficult to find in a dish made in a short period of time. Divide the couscous among four large serving plates or shallow soup bowls. Place the squabs on top, pour the sauce over, and garnish with the cilantro leaves and sesame seeds. If you like, serve it with bulgur or basmati rice instead of couscous, accompanied by steamed haricots verts or small sweet peas tossed with cardamom and butter.

meats and large game

Unlike poultry and fish cookery, the way meats are prepared around the Mediterranean Rim, from the Italian grilled veal chop to the Moroccan lamb tagine, is so varied that the rules are not hard and fast. The numerous types as well as cuts of meat create an almost endless array of possibilities. If you want to have lamb, for example, you must first choose the cut before deciding how to cook it. Lamb shanks require braising for a long period over low heat until this tough cut softens. My Braised Lamb Shank with Dried Apricots cooks for well over an hour, until the meat falls off the bone. On the other hand, the tender rib chops in Lamb Chops Marinated in Cardamom and Yogurt cook in a matter of minutes over high heat.

Lamb is my favorite meat because it is the most versatile. Besides shanks and chops, chunks of lamb (usually from the shoulder) can be stewed, as in the Lamb Tagine with Dried Figs and Almonds. Ground lamb can be used in a casserole like the Moussaka with Zucchini, for a filling as in the Spicy Lamb Dumplings (page 29), or in Kibbeh with Spiced Pumpkin (page 32).

Roasted Pork Loin with Pistachio and Dried Apricot Stuffing, and Olive Oil Mashed Potatoes

Lamb is used all along the Mediterranean Rim, responding equally well to the complex spice blends of North Africa and to the more straightforward garlic and herbs of Italy or Greece. Lamb has an almost gamey quality—more evident in tender cuts like loin and rib chops than in the tougher shoulders and shanks—so it can handle heavy seasoning and sweet sauces or accompaniments like chutneys. While I consider mint jelly an abomination, mint is a good accompaniment to lamb, but only as a fresh herb or in a chutney. Other seasonings I like with lamb are cardamom, cumin, cinnamon, cloves, saffron, garlic, rosemary, and thyme.

Due to religious beliefs in Israel and the Muslim countries on the Mediterranean Rim, pork is not as common in the area as a whole, though it used often in Italy, France, and Spain and somewhat less frequently in Greece. Italy probably reigns supreme in its use of pork in everything from stuffed pig's feet (zampone) to loins pot-roasted in milk. Unfortunately, Americans have two problems when cooking pork. First, fear of trichinosis has caused many to overcook pork, robbing it of moisture and flavor. Since the trichina worm is killed at about 140 degrees, it's silly to cook pork to 170 or 180 degrees as some old cookbooks recommend. A cooking temperature of 150 to 155 degrees will provide a measure of safety while keeping the pork moist with a touch of pink (though I like my pork even less well done).

The second problem is the tendency to go overboard with cloying, syrupy glazes and sauces like barbecue sauces for ribs and Southern-style barbecue and sugary coatings for baked ham. While it's true that pork's natural sweetness lends itself to sweeter preparations than beef, for example, a light hand is needed so the essentially delicate flavor of the meat is not overwhelmed. I use dried fruits like apricots, figs, dates, and prunes, as you will note in the Roasted Pork Loin with Pistachio and Dried Apricot Stuffing. With these sweeter presentations, spices such as cinnamon, cumin, cardamom, and allspice are most appropriate. Mustard and garlic offer contrasts to pork's sweetness. Other pork-friendly seasonings are fennel, rosemary, and sage.

Though beef is more abundant in the United States than it is on the Mediterranean Rim, the way beef is cooked in America more closely approximates the way it is cooked in the Mediterranean than any other meat. In both cases, simple preparations like pan-frying and grilling are favored. This means any flavors infused into the beef must be quick and straightforward. The famous Italian bistecca alla fiorentina (grilled T-bone steak) has nothing more added to it than salt, a grinding of black pepper, and a brush of olive oil. We've tried some fancy preparations with beef at Matthew's, but to no avail. Though we are eating leaner cuts of beef, the meat-and-potatoes mindset of Americans is unshakable. My Spicy Beef with Tomato Jam is about as far as most of my customers will go.

Aside from Italy, which uses a great deal of it, and France, which uses it moderately, veal is not widely consumed along the Mediterranean Rim. Cooking veal with dry-heat methods requires a deft hand because it can easily be overcooked and become dry. Marinades are another way to help prevent meat from drying out, as in the Grilled Veal Chops in Red Onion Marinade.

Veal is also essentially a bland meat. So you need seasonings that perk up the dish but not so strongly that they obliterate the delicate nature of the meat. I prefer simple veal dishes, occasionally with pungent flavors (though in moderation) such as olives, capers, and lemon-based sauces. A good example is veal piccata in which lemons and capers are in perfect balance. Other good veal seasonings are sage, rosemary, and garlic. Stronger or more complex seasoning might be used in braised dishes like osso buco.

Because of advanced farming methods and rapid transportation, game isn't as exotic as it once was. Now, thanks to companies like D'Artagnan, we can avail ourselves of wild boar, venison, and hare. While I have no recipes for wild boar or hare in this book, both are hunted widely around the Mediterranean Rim.

Venison is probably the most common game. And 80 to 85 percent of our venison—mostly red deer native to Europe—is farm-raised in New Zealand. Domestic venison is less common and not as uniform in terms of cuts and sizes. Truly wild domestic venison, which cannot be legally sold, is less tender and has a gamier flavor than most farm-raised venison. Though I've hunted deer since I was ten years old, I prefer farm-raised venison because of its consistency, flavor, and tenderness. Yet it is still strong enough to tolerate strong seasonings like those in the Loin of Venison in Black Pepper Pomegranate Marinade as well as spices like juniper, earthy seasonings like olives, nuts, and grains, and rich, fortified wines like port and marsala. Citrus flavors such as orange or lemon are also good with venison in either a marinade—like the Spiced Venison Salad with Blood Orange Marinade (page 49)—sauce, vinaigrette, or chutney.

Because venison is so lean, it is imperative not to overcook it. It should never be more than medium-rare, preferably rare. Otherwise, the meat will be tough and dry. Because venison and other game evoke the flavors of fall and winter, I like to accompany them with vegetables of that season: sweet potatoes, squash, turnips, and other root vegetables.

One final note about shopping for meat. While supermarkets do a better job with meat than they do with seafood, I still think seeking out a good butcher is a good idea. You will pay a little more but you will get higher quality meats. Supermarkets rarely have grades higher than choice, and many markets often sell even lower grades. I prefer prime beef to Certified Black Angus, though the latter has its followers. In addition to carrying a better selection of meats, a butcher will give you service that is tailored to your needs, not the one-size-fits-all treatment you get in most supermarkets.

Loin of Venison in Black Pepper–Pomegranate Marinade

braised lamb shank with dried apricots

serves 4

This dish brings together the two ends of the Mediterranean Rim. The spices are Moroccan but the lamb shank is very Greek. Serve with couscous and a green vegetable like asparagus.

½ cup sesame seeds
3 tablespoons cumin seeds
3 tablespoons coriander seeds
4 lamb shanks (12 to 14 ounces each), trimmed of excess fat
Salt and freshly ground black pepper
¼ cup olive oil
2 carrots, chopped
2 ribs celery, chopped
1 piece fresh ginger (1 inch), chopped
1 large Spanish onion, grated
Large pinch of saffron
1 cup white wine
1 cinnamon stick
1 teaspoon ground ginger
1 ½ teaspoons ground cloves
2 bay leaves
1 cup whole dried apricots
4 cups Chicken Stock (page 15)
¼ cup chopped dried apricots
1 tablespoon butter

Preheat the oven to 350 degrees. Put the sesame seeds on a small sheet pan or pie plate and toast for 14 to 15 minutes, or until golden brown. Set aside. Meanwhile, toast the cumin seeds in a skillet for 4 minutes, stirring a few times. Grind the cumin and coriander seeds with a mortar and pestle or in a spice grinder. Set aside.

Season the shanks with salt and pepper. Put the olive oil in a large flameproof roasting pan over medium-high heat. Brown the shanks on all sides, 10 to 15 minutes.

Remove the shanks, pour off the fat, and add the carrots and celery. Cook over medium heat for 4 to 5 minutes, or until just beginning to soften. Add the fresh ginger, onion, and saffron and cook until the onion is translucent and soft, about 5 minutes. Add the wine, cumin, coriander, cinnamon stick, ground ginger, ground cloves, bay leaves, and whole dried apricots. Cook for 5 minutes.

Place the shanks back in the pan and add the stock. Cover the pan and cook in the oven for about 1½ hours, or until the meat is tender and falling off the bone. Remove the lamb and keep it warm, covered with foil.

Skim the fat and strain the liquid into a saucepan. Discard the solids. Reduce the braising liquid to a saucy consistency by slowly simmering. Time will vary widely; it may take as long as 15 to 20 minutes. Adjust the seasoning with salt and pepper. Add the chopped apricots and butter.

To serve the lamb, coat with the sauce and sprinkle with sesame seeds.

lamb chops marinated in cardamom and yogurt

serves 4

Yogurt in marinades is as common in the Mediterranean Rim as sheep grazing on a hillside, so it's not surprising that this kind of marinade is often used with lamb. It produces three distinct characteristics. First, the proteins in yogurt act as a tenderizer. Second, the yogurt rounds out the richness of lamb, softening what for some is a strong lamby flavor. And third, when caramelized during cooking, the yogurt adds another flavor dimension. Smoky is the best way I can describe it. This marinade can also be used with venison or squab.

1 cup plain yogurt
¼ cup fresh lemon juice
1 tablespoon ground dried chilies such as ancho, or chili powder
2 ½ tablespoons ground cardamom
½ cup olive oil
12 rib lamb chops (about 4 ounces each)
Salt and freshly ground black pepper
½ cup Tahini-Yogurt Sauce (page 158) (optional)
½ cup Mint Chutney (page 155) (optional)
¼ cup cilantro leaves

Mix the yogurt, lemon juice, ground chilies, cardamom and ¼ cup of the olive oil in a shallow nonreactive (glass, enamel, or ceramic) dish large enough to hold all the lamb chops tightly in 1 layer. Add the lamb chops, cover, and refrigerate for 6 to 24 hours, turning once.

Remove the lamb from the marinade, scraping off any marinade from the chops. Season with salt and pepper and brush with 2 tablespoons of the remaining oil. Put the last 2 tablespoons of oil in a large heavy-bottomed skillet over medium-high heat. Cook the chops 3 to 4 minutes per side for medium-rare. Lamb should be slightly springy to the touch and the juices reddish pink. You will have to do this in batches. Cover cooked chops with foil to keep warm. Allow the chops to rest for 3 to 4 minutes.

Arrange 3 chops on each of 4 plates, overlapping in a semicircle. Drizzle with Mint Chutney or Tahini-Yogurt Sauce, if desired, and garnish with cilantro leaves on top.

Serve with Tunisian Couscous Salad (page 39).

moussaka with zucchini

serves 6 to 8

Traditional moussaka, made with eggplant, can be heavy and greasy. This version with zucchini is lighter. Thinly sliced potatoes can be used instead of zucchini. Beef may be substituted for lamb.

½ cup plus 1 tablespoon olive oil
1 pound ground lamb
2 medium onions, sliced ⅛ inch thick
2 cloves garlic, thinly sliced
2 tablespoons ground cinnamon
2 tablespoons nutmeg
¼ teaspoon cayenne
½ cup chopped parsley
2 tablespoons fresh oregano leaves, chopped, or 2 teaspoons dried oregano
2 large tomatoes, peeled, seeded, and chopped (see page 17)
Salt and freshly ground black pepper
3 medium zucchini, cut crosswise into ½-inch-thick slices
4 tablespoons unsalted butter
½ cup all-purpose flour
1 ¾ cups hot low-fat milk
2 egg yolks
⅔ cup grated parmesan

Put ¼ cup of the oil in a large skillet over medium heat. Add the lamb and brown, 8 to 10 minutes. Add the onions, garlic, 1 tablespoon of the cinnamon, 1 tablespoon of the nutmeg, and the cayenne. Reduce the heat to medium and cook for 8 to 10 minutes, or until onions are golden. Add the parsley, oregano, tomatoes, salt, and pepper. Stir and cook for 1 minute, then pour into a bowl and set aside.

Wipe out the skillet, add ¼ cup of the remaining oil, and sauté one-third of the zucchini over medium-high heat, 4 to 6 minutes. Repeat with the remaining zucchini 2 more times. Drain zucchini on paper towels.

Melt the butter in a heavy saucepan over medium-low heat. Stir in the flour, the remaining 1 tablespoon cinnamon, the remaining 1 tablespoon nutmeg, and salt and pepper. Cook for 3 to 4 minutes. Whisk in the milk, bring to a boil over medium-high heat, then reduce the heat. Simmer, uncovered, for 20 minutes, stirring 3 or 4 times. Strain into a bowl and whisk in the eggs and parmesan. Taste for salt and pepper.

Preheat the oven to 400 degrees. Brush a 10 x 7 x 2-inch baking dish with the remaining tablespoon of olive oil. Arrange half of the zucchini in 1 layer on the bottom, slightly overlapping. Spread the meat mixture over, then add another layer of zucchini. Cover with the white sauce and bake for 20 to 24 minutes. The top should be golden brown. Let rest for 10 minutes, then cut into squares.

lamb tagine with dried figs and almonds

serves 4

Although I love the flavor of most tagines—Moroccan stews cooked in an earthenware pot with a conical cover—I find the texture of many to be mushy and one-dimensional. What makes this tagine unique is the crisp top it achieves from the final baking step. This is a great party or buffet dish because it can be prepared ahead right up to the point at which it goes into the oven to crisp the top. Rich and filling, this tagine needs nothing more than a salad or grilled vegetables to turn it into a satisfying meal.

¼ cup sesame seeds
½ cup sliced almonds
2 tablespoons olive oil
2 ½ pounds boned lamb shoulder, trimmed of excess fat and cut into 1 ½-inch cubes
Salt and freshly ground black pepper
2 cloves garlic, minced
1 medium onion, chopped
1 teaspoon ground cumin
1 teaspoon ground cardamom
1 teaspoon turmeric
1 teaspoon ground dried chili peppers such as ancho, or chili powder
1 cup dried figs, quartered
4 tablespoons chopped cilantro plus 8 sprigs of cilantro

Preheat the oven to 350 degrees. Put the sesame seeds on a small sheet pan or pie plate and toast in the oven 6 minutes. Add the almonds and toast another 8 to 9 minutes until golden brown. Set aside.

Put the olive oil in a large, heavy-bottomed Dutch oven over medium-high heat. Season the lamb with salt and pepper. Brown on all sides in 2 batches, about 10 to 12 minutes total. Add the garlic, onions, cumin, cardamom, turmeric, and ground chilies to the lamb. Stir well and reduce the heat to medium-low. Cook for 5 minutes. Add 2⅔ cups water and bring to a boil. Reduce the heat, cover, and simmer for 1½ hours, or until the meat is tender. It should be slightly springy, but easy to pull apart with your fingers.

Preheat the oven to 425 degrees.

Strain the liquid from the stew into a small saucepan or bowl and skim the fat. Check for salt and pepper and keep warm. Mix the meat and figs and spread in a single layer in an ovenproof serving dish. Pour the sauce over the meat and figs and sprinkle with almonds. Bake for 12 minutes, or until crisp and golden.

Sprinkle with sesame seeds and chopped cilantro and garnish with cilantro sprigs. Serve from the hot dish.

roasted pork loin with pistachio and dried apricot stuffing

serves 6

Dried apricots and pistachios are often used in the eastern Mediterranean, especially in Turkey. Apricots have a subtle sweetness that enhances but does not drown out pork's delicate flavor. Pistachios add a gentle counterpoint. Other dried fruit and nut combinations are: golden raisins and walnuts, figs and almonds, and dates and hazelnuts. Though butterflying the loin is quite simple, have the butcher do it if you're not comfortable doing it yourself. Serve with Olive Oil Mashed Potatoes (page 125) and Broccoli Raab with Almonds and Hot Pepper (page 119).

⅔ cup blanched pistachios
½ cup dried apricots
Kosher salt and freshly ground black pepper
1 boneless loin of pork (3 pounds), with a thin layer of fat on the outside
2 tablespoons minced garlic
1 tablespoon minced ginger
3 tablespoons olive oil
1 tablespoon minced fresh rosemary
2 tablespoons cumin seeds
½ cup Rich Chicken Stock (page 16)
1 tablespoon honey
1 tablespoon fresh lemon juice
2 tablespoons minced chives

Preheat the oven to 350 degrees. Put the pistachios on a small sheet pan or pie plate and toast for 11 minutes, or until browned but not too dark. Remove and coarsely chop. Set aside.

Bring 2 cups of water to a boil in a small saucepan. Add the dried apricots, remove the pan from the heat, and allow the apricots to soften for 10 minutes. Drain and cut apricots into ¼-inch dice. Put the apricots in a small bowl with the pistachios, ½ teaspoon salt, and ¼ teaspoon pepper. Set aside.

Butterfly the pork loin by making a lengthwise incision from the top of the loin all the way through the meat to within ½ inch of the bottom. Spread open the cut meat. In a small bowl, mix the garlic, ginger, oil, rosemary, ½ teaspoon salt, and ¼ teaspoon pepper. Rub the inside of the pork with the garlic-ginger mixture.

Evenly spread the apricot-pistachio mixture inside the loin. Close up the meat and tie it tightly with string both crosswise and lengthwise. Spread the cumin seeds on a cutting board or platter and roll the loin in the seeds.

Place the pork loin on a rack in a roasting pan and cover with foil. Cook for 1 hour and 20 minutes. Remove the foil and cook for 20 minutes longer, or until the center is pink and the internal temperature is 150 degrees. Cover and let rest at room temperature for 15 minutes.

Meanwhile, bring the stock, honey, and lemon juice to a boil in a small saucepan and reduce to ¼ cup, 5 to 8 minutes. Adjust the salt and pepper as needed. Keep warm.

Cut the pork crosswise into ½-inch slices. Place 2 slices on each of 6 plates. If any filling falls out, sprinkle it on top of the slices. Drizzle with the sauce and sprinkle with chives.

spicy beef with tomato jam

serves 4

1 cup Tomato Jam (page 153)
2 tablespoons fresh lemon juice
2 shallots, chopped
1 clove garlic, chopped
1 fresh chili pepper, such as jalapeño or serrano, stemmed, seeded, and chopped, or 1 ½ tablespoons ground dried ancho chilies
4 top sirloin steaks, 1 inch thick (6 to 8 ounces each)
¼ cup olive oil
Kosher salt
¼ cup coarsely chopped cilantro leaves

In a blender or food processor, puree ½ cup of the jam with the lemon juice, shallots, garlic, and chili pepper until smooth.

Place the steaks in 1 layer in a glass dish or baking dish and coat all sides with the marinade. Cover and refrigerate for 6 to 24 hours.

Put the olive oil in a large heavy skillet over high heat. Remove the steaks from the marinade and brown for 1 minute per side. Continue cooking while turning the steaks every minute, a total of 8 minutes, 4 minutes per side. Remove from the heat and let rest for 3 to 4 minutes on a cutting board.

To serve, cut the steaks against the grain into ⅛-inch-thick slices. Sprinkle with salt and divide among 4 plates, overlapping the slices. Drizzle with the remaining ½ cup of jam and sprinkle with chopped cilantro.

Whether it's a Neapolitan steak pizzaiola or a good old American hamburger, beef has a certain affinity for tomatoes. I think it's because the acid in the tomatoes cuts the richness of the beef. My Tomato Jam has an added benefit. It caramelizes as the beef sears, providing a shiny, sweet, and spicy veneer for the meat. And you can use it on hamburgers if you run out of ketchup.

grilled veal chops in red onion marinade

serves 4

Veal can overcook and become dry very quickly, so as a protective measure, I often use a light marinade like the one in this recipe. The flavors in the marinade are almost universal to the Mediterranean Rim and can be used for beef, pork, and lamb as well. Serve with Toasted Barley Risotto with Wild Mushrooms (page 62).

3 tablespoons Spicy Olive Oil (page 13)
1 small red onion, minced
½ teaspoon minced ginger
2 cloves garlic, minced
¼ teaspoon coarsely cracked coriander seeds
½ teaspoon coarsely cracked black pepper
4 bay leaves
2 tablespoons sherry vinegar
½ cup white wine
4 rib veal chops, about 1½ inches thick (14 ounces each)
Salt
2 tablespoons chopped parsley

Put the olive oil in a small saucepan over medium heat for a few minutes just until it gets warm. In a heatproof bowl, mix the onion, ginger, and garlic. Add the warm olive oil. Let steep for 10 minutes. Add the coriander, pepper, bay leaves, vinegar, and white wine. Let cool to room temperature. The marinade can be prepared up to 24 hours in advance and stored, covered, in the refrigerator.

Place the veal chops in a baking dish about 2 inches deep and just large enough to hold the chops tightly in 1 layer. Pour the marinade over them and turn to coat well. Cover and marinate in the refrigerator 6 to 10 hours.

If grilling, prepare a charcoal or gas grill with the grate 4 inches from the heat source. Preheat the oven to 400 degrees.

Remove the chops from marinade at least 30 minutes before cooking and season with salt. Grill the chops about 6 minutes on each side, brushing with the marinade every 2 minutes. Or sear the chops about 4 minutes on each side in a large sauté pan over medium-high heat. Place the grilled or seared chops in a baking pan and put in the oven for 4 minutes, or until the center of the meat is medium-rare. Juices should be pale pink, and the meat soft with some resistance to the touch. The chops may also be broiled 4 inches from the heat source for 7 to 8 minutes per side. Do not put the broiled chops into the oven.

Allow the meat to rest for 5 minutes before serving. Sprinkle with chopped parsley.

loin of venison in black pepper–pomegranate marinade

serves 6

2 large onions, coarsely chopped
1 piece of fresh ginger (about 1 inch), coarsely chopped
½ orange (unpeeled), seeded and cut into ½-inch chunks
2 tablespoons coarsely ground black pepper
1 ½ cups pomegranate juice or 1 cup pinot noir with 2 tablespoons pomegranate molasses (see page 14)
1 clove garlic, coarsely chopped
Pinch of ground allspice
1 boneless loin of venison (about 3 pounds)
2 tablespoons olive oil
Salt
2 tablespoons chopped chives

In a blender, puree the onions, ginger, orange, black pepper, pomegranate juice, garlic, and allspice. Cut the venison crosswise into 12 medallions. Lay the medallions flat in 1 layer in a nonreactive (glass, enamel, or ceramic) dish and pour the marinade over. Turn to coat well, cover, and refrigerate 24 to 36 hours.

Remove the venison from the marinade and wipe off excess marinade with a paper towel. Put the olive oil in a large skillet over medium-high heat. Or use 2 skillets, each with 2 tablespoons of oil. Season the venison with salt and cook the medallions 2½ for minutes per side. Meat should be medium-rare, with plenty of red in the center.

To serve, place 2 medallions on each plate and sprinkle with chives.

Serve with Spinach with White Raisins and Capers (page 126).

Pomegranates are used frequently in the eastern Mediterranean (as well as Morocco) in everything from breakfast drinks to salads. The lively sweet-tart quality of the fruit's juice is also good as a marinade with strong meats like lamb and game like venison. Venison and other lean cuts of meat benefit from marinating because the marinade is in direct contact with the meat, unencumbered by fat or skin. Thus the marinade penetrates easily and provides flavor that the fat normally would.

vegetables and side dishes

Vegetables and side dishes have long been an after-thought in America. When you asked Mom what was for dinner, the answer was invariably some-thing like roast beef or fried chicken or meat loaf, not fried chicken with Cardamon-Baked Sweet Potatoes, and Charcoal-Grilled Asparagus with Warm Sourdough Croutons. Vegetables were hardly mentioned at all unless they were aligned with the meat or protein of the meal, as in fish and chips. And when you did get them, the vegetables were more often than not overcooked and underseasoned.

Around the Mediterranean, vegetables are featured more prominently and given more interesting treatments. At Mezze, my casual Mediter-ranean Rim café, about 80 percent of the menu is meatless. I couldn't do that if I cooked vegetables the old-fashioned American way.

Artichokes Braised with Coriander, Lemon, and Garlic

The Moroccan Spiced Carrots a good example of what I mean. The carrots are first seared in olive oil. This provides an interesting charred color and caramelization. Then the heat is lowered and the carrots are cooked without water so that the flavor and nutrients aren't washed down the drain. Nor are the seasonings used in the Moroccan Spiced Carrots often seen in American side dishes or vegetable preparations. They give the dish a rich flavor that you might normally expect only in the entree of the meal.

Even a vegetable as simple as baked sweet potatoes can be raised to new heights with cardamom and chili powder, as in Cardamom-Baked Sweet Potatoes. Anise seeds and olive oil do the same for that American favorite, mashed potatoes, in Olive Oil Mashed Potatoes.

Other flavorings for vegetables include onions, garlic, toasted nuts, toasted bread crumbs, raisins and other dried fruit, capers, olives, fresh herbs, crushed red pepper, freshly squeezed fruit juices, freshly toasted and ground spices such as anise, cumin, cardamom, and coriander, honey and other sweeteners like pomegranate molasses, and flavored oils such as nut oils. (And even though they are not specifically used in this book, I like oils infused with wild mushrooms, herbs, and garlic.)

Sweetness is a common theme in vegetable preparations along the Mediterranean Rim as in the Pomegranate-Glazed Eggplant. Sweet-and-sour flavors are even more complex, and they are very common in southern Italian cooking. The Spinach with Raisins and Capers achieves that effect simply by combining the sweet raisins and sour capers with the spinach. For a more complicated technique, see how the onions are cooked in the Crisp Red Snapper with Onion Agrodolce (page 72).

Another major difference between Mediterranean Rim and American vegetable cookery is that olive oil is used instead of butter. Oil is not merely added when the vegetables are cooked but it is also used as a cooking medium. When used as a dressing, the oil is sometimes combined with lemon juice or another acid and the cooked vegetables are tossed in this mixture. When the dressing is added while the vegetables are still hot—a common Mediterranean Rim technique used in the Moroccan Spiced Carrots—flavors soak in more deeply.

The ways in which vegetables are cooked are almost as varied as the vegetables themselves. Instead of limiting yourself to steaming or boiling vegetables, try grilling them, oven roasting at high temperatures, and sautéing. Grilling, as in Grilled Zucchini with Almonds and Tomato Jam, is a great way to add more flavor without a lot of fat. So as not to char the outside before the inside of the vegetable cooks, you may need to blanch the vegetables first, a technique I use in Charcoal-Grilled Asparagus with Warm Sourdough Croutons. Many restaurants blanch vegetables ahead of time, then refresh them in ice water. Later the vegetables are reheated by grilling, or sautéing them in oil with herbs and spices. The best vegetables to handle in this fashion are green beans and asparagus.

Though I advocate complex flavors in vegetable and side dishes, I still believe the preparations themselves should be rather simple. This approach allows you to prepare several dishes rather than one or two—and even to make a meal out of them, something I often do.

The flavors in vegetable side dishes should complement the flavors in the main dish. For example, a fish dish with robust flavors like Tuna with Almond-Sesame Crust (page 76) should be paired with a mild vegetable like the Grilled Asparagus, rather than a more intensely flavored side dish like the Spiced Carrots. On the other hand, those carrots would be perfect with a simple mixed grill.

When choosing what vegetables to cook, I use much of the same logic I've discussed in the Seafood and Salad chapters. That is to stick with produce in season and to pick the best that is available at the market that day—regardless of what your shopping list says. I recommend you buy organic produce if you can, at local farmers' markets, supermarkets, and natural or whole foods stores that feature organic produce.

As to specific vegetables, I use Idaho potatoes for mashing, red-skinned potatoes for roasting, and white creamers or Yukon Gold potatoes for boiling. With other vegetables, I like smaller rather than larger sizes, though I'm not especially fond of baby vegetables. Large carrots, for example, are often woody and not as sweet as smaller carrots. Smaller zucchini are more tender and less fibrous than larger ones. For eggplant, lighter is better than heavier because it means fewer seeds, which can make the eggplant bitter.

Though convenient, I avoid spinach in bags. I like the sense of connection with the earth that spinach and other leafy green vegetables with stems and clinging dirt gives me. The downside is that dirt must be scrupulously cleaned in several changes of cool water to get rid of sand and grit.

Finally, a word about texture, as important in my vegetables as it is in the rest of my food. That's why I added croutons to asparagus in Charcoal-Grilled Asparagus with Warm Sourdough Croutons and toasted bread crumbs to the Spinach with Golden Raisins and Capers. Nuts also add a welcome crunch to vegetable preparations, like the pine nuts in the Moroccan Spiced Carrots. Toasted hazelnuts and almonds are also good additions to vegetable dishes.

serves 4

artichokes braised with coriander, lemon, and garlic

Braised vegetable dishes are versatile because they can be prepared in advance and reheated or eaten cold or at room temperature. These artichokes could be served with almost any type of lamb dish, game bird, or a roasted chicken. It could be part of a mezze or antipasto table. Or it could be part of a salad with greens like chicory, endive, or escarole, some olives, and parmesan or pecorino cheese. If you do it this way, use some of the braising liquid in the salad dressing.

¼ cup fresh lemon juice
12 baby artichokes
⅔ cup dry white wine
⅔ cup extra virgin olive oil
4 cloves garlic, each peeled and sliced lengthwise into 3 pieces
3 tablespoons coarsely cracked coriander seeds
Grated zest of 1 lemon (about 1 tablespoon)
12 mint leaves, stacked, rolled (if large enough), and cut crosswise into thin ribbons.
2 tablespoons small capers, drained
Salt and freshly ground black pepper

In a large bowl, combine 2 tablespoons of the lemon juice with 4 cups cold water. Trim ¼ inch from the tops of the artichokes, cut off ¼ inch of the stem and remove the tough outer leaves near the bottom. Slice in half lengthwise. Remove the inner choke if the artichokes are large. (If the artichokes are small, there is no need to do so.) Add to the lemon water.

Drain the artichokes and place in a large nonreactive (stainless steel or enameled) saucepan with the white wine, olive oil, garlic, coriander seeds, and zest. Bring to a boil, then reduce to a simmer. Cover and cook for about 20 minutes, or until the artichokes are tender when pierced by a fork. Add the mint, capers, remaining 2 tablespoons lemon juice, and salt and pepper.

Remove the artichokes with a slotted spoon and place in a deep bowl or casserole dish. Spoon ¼ cup of the liquid over the artichokes and serve warm or at room temperature.

broccoli raab with almonds and hot pepper

serves 4

2/3 cup sliced almonds
Salt
1 large bunch broccoli raab (about 1 pound), 1/2 inch of stem bottoms and any damaged or yellowed leaves removed
3 tablespoons Spicy Olive Oil (page 13)
2 cloves garlic, chopped
1/2 teaspoon crushed red pepper

Preheat the oven to 350 degrees. Put the sliced almonds on a small sheet pan or pie plate and toast in the oven for 8 to 9 minutes, or until golden brown. Set aside.

Meanwhile, bring a pot with 4 quarts of water and 1 tablespoon salt to a rapid boil. Add the broccoli raab and cook for 3 minutes. Drain in a colander and cool under cold running water. Drain well and remove to a cutting board. Roughly chop into approximately 3/4-inch pieces.

Put the oil a large skillet over medium heat. Add the garlic, cook for 30 seconds, and add the broccoli raab. Cook for 3 to 4 minutes, add the red pepper and toss to mix well. Remove from the heat, add the almonds, and toss well. Season with salt to taste and serve hot in a large bowl.

The techniques in this recipe—that is, blanching and refreshing, then finishing by sautéing, grilling, or roasting—can be used with other green vegetables such as asparagus and green beans. You can also turn this side vegetable into a pasta dish by using a well-textured pasta like cavatelli (short curled pasta), fusilli (corkscrews), or radiatori (radiators), which allows bits of almond to get stuck in the nooks and crannies of the pasta.

charcoal-grilled asparagus with warm sourdough croutons

serves 4

Asparagus is a vegetable that demands simple preparation. Gentle grilling brings out its natural sweetness; oven roasting will achieve nearly the same results. Croutons on the grill is an unusual touch, but I'm so fond of them, warm and crisp and soaked with olive oil, they're the first thing I eat.

Ice water
20 jumbo asparagus spears
¼ cup extra virgin olive oil
16 cubes (each 1 inch square) of sourdough bread, crusts removed
Salt and freshly ground black pepper
1 piece (4 ounces) parmesan
3 tablespoons chopped chives
¼ cup Cilantro Dressing (page 79)

Put a pot with 2 quarts of water on to boil. Have a large bowl of ice water ready. Cut off 1 to 1½ inches from the woody bottom of each asparagus spear. Peel the bottom 3 inches. When the water boils, add the asparagus and cook for 3 minutes. Remove the spears and plunge into the ice water until cooled, about 5 minutes. Drain well.

Heat a charcoal grill, gas grill, or broiler. Toss the olive oil, bread cubes, asparagus, and salt and pepper in a mixing bowl. Grill the asparagus and croutons until charred but not blackened, about 4 minutes.

After grilling, toss the asparagus and croutons with any oil left in the bowl. Arrange croutons and asparagus on a plate. With a vegetable peeler, shave parmesan over the asparagus. Drizzle with Cilantro Dressing. Garnish with chives and additional pepper.

moroccan spiced carrots

serves 4

Carrots are a pretty durable vegetable that can handle a fair amount of seasoning as I found out when, on a 1994 trip to Morocco with other chefs, I was handed some carrots and a bunch of spices and told to whip up something. The result was a dish that has become the most popular dish at Mezze.

2 tablespoons pine nuts
1 ½ tablespoons cumin seeds
¼ cup olive oil
12 medium carrots, trimmed, peeled, and cut on the diagonal into ⅛-inch-thick slices
½ teaspoon kosher salt
1 tablespoon honey
4 teaspoons fresh lemon juice
12 Moroccan or other black oil-cured olives, pitted and chopped
1 tablespoon chopped cilantro
2 teaspoons chopped fresh mint

Preheat the oven to 350 degrees. Put the pine nuts on a small sheet pan or pie plate and toast for 9 to 10 minutes, or until golden brown. Set aside. Meanwhile, put the cumin seeds in a heavy skillet over medium heat and toast for 4 minutes, stirring a few times. Grind in a mortar and pestle or spice grinder. Set aside.

Put the olive oil in a skillet large enough to hold the carrots in 1 layer. Cook the carrots over high heat for about 3 minutes. Lower the heat to medium and cook for 2 minutes more, or until the carrots are tender and golden brown. Gently shake the pan to cook evenly. Add the salt.

Put the carrots in a colander to drain. Transfer carrots to a mixing bowl. Add the honey, lemon juice, olives, and cumin and mix together. Cool to room temperature and mix in the cilantro, mint, and pine nuts. To serve, place in a large decorative bowl.

serves 4

pomegranate-glazed eggplant

The tart, syrupy quality of pomegranate molasses, which is a reduction of pomegranate juice, is ideal for glazing meats, fish, and, in this case, vegetables. The glaze helps to keep the eggplant from drying out, and the sweetness of the molasses counteracts any potential bitterness.

2 medium eggplants (about 1 pound each)
2 teaspoons kosher salt
2 tablespoons sugar
¼ cup olive oil
1 clove garlic, minced
1 medium onion, chopped
2 ripe medium tomatoes, peeled, seeded, and chopped (see page 17)
¼ teaspoon crushed red pepper
¼ cup pomegranate molasses (see page 14)
¼ cup basil leaves, cut into julienne strips, plus 2 tablespoons julienned leaves (optional) for garnish
2 tablespoons coarsely chopped cilantro plus 2 tablespoons (optional) chopped cilantro for garnish
Salt and freshly ground black pepper
¼ cup pomegranate seeds (optional)

Remove about 1 inch from the top of each eggplant and stand each upright. Slice down on 4 sides of the eggplant, creating 4 slices, each about ½ inch thick with the skin intact. Reserve the center of the eggplant for another use. Cut each slice crosswise into ¼-inch-wide slices, creating half-moons. Toss them with the kosher salt and sugar and drain in a colander for 30 minutes. Pat dry with paper towels.

Put 2 tablespoons of the olive oil in a medium skillet over medium-high heat. Add half of the eggplant and fry until golden brown on all sides, 4 to 5 minutes. Transfer to a plate lined with paper towels using a slotted spoon. Repeat with the remaining 2 tablespoons oil and eggplant. Leave any oil in the skillet (there won't be much).

Reduce the heat under the skillet to medium, add the garlic and onion and cook for 2 to 3 minutes. Add the tomatoes and red pepper and cook for 5 minutes. Add the eggplant to the tomato-onion mixture.

Turn the heat to high and add the pomegranate molasses. Cook until the liquid coats the eggplant and is slightly shiny, 3 to 4 minutes. Transfer the mixture to a mixing bowl and allow to cool for 10 minutes. Stir in the basil and cilantro and season with salt and black pepper. Let rest for 1 hour at room temperature.

Transfer the eggplant to a colorful bowl and sprinkle with pomegranate seeds and additional basil or cilantro, if desired.

olive oil mashed potatoes

serves 4

1 teaspoon anise seeds
Salt
2 pounds creamers (small white or red potatoes) or new potatoes, peeled
⅓ cup extra virgin olive oil, warm or at room temperature
White pepper, preferably freshly ground

Put the anise seeds in a heavy skillet over medium heat. Toast for 4 minutes, stirring a few times. Grind with a mortar and pestle or in a spice grinder. Set aside.

Meanwhile, in large saucepan, combine 2 quarts of water with 1 tablespoon salt. Bring to a boil, add the potatoes and cook, covered, for 20 to 25 minutes, or until tender. Drain.

While still hot, run the potatoes through a food mill into a large mixing bowl. Or use a ricer or hand masher. Do not use a food processor. Stir in the olive oil, ground anise, and salt and pepper to taste. Pour into a colorful serving bowl to offset the white of the potatoes.

For people who put butter in their mashed potatoes, the olive oil in this dish will be a revelation. And for those who season their mashed potatoes only with salt and pepper, the toasted anise seeds will be even more startling. To prevent the potatoes from becoming too thick and pasty, the olive oil must be warm or at room temperature when added to the potatoes. Mashed potatoes with olive oil don't hold up as well as traditional mashed potatoes —they seize up and harden more quickly—so they must be eaten hot.

spinach with white raisins and capers

serves 4 to 6

I like to hide things within the leaves of spinach to give the diner a surprise. In this dish, the surprise is a sweet-and-sour combo of raisins and capers. Combined with garlic, tomato, and toasted bread crumbs, they make the spinach enticing. One particular note about cooking spinach: Many cooks are so concerned about overcooking, they wind up undercooking it. The result is spinach with an unpleasant furry film on the leaves.

Salt
Ice water
1 ½ pounds spinach
3 tablespoons olive oil
1 tomato, peeled, seeded, and chopped (see page 17)
2 cloves garlic, minced
4 teaspoons capers, drained
¼ cup golden (sultana) raisins, plumped in warm water for about 20 minutes
¼ cup coarse Toasted Bread Crumbs (recipe follows)
Freshly ground black pepper

Bring a large pot with 2 quarts of water and 1 teaspoon salt to a boil. Have a bowl of ice water ready. Meanwhile, trim the stems of the spinach and wash thoroughly in 3 changes of cool water to remove sand and grit. Drain. Blanch the spinach in the boiling water for 1 minute. Drain and plunge into the ice water. Drain, squeeze out excess moisture, and coarsely chop.

Heat the olive oil in a large sauté pan over medium-high heat. Add the tomato and cook for 4 to 5 minutes. Add the garlic and spinach and reduce the heat to medium. Cook for an additional 3 minutes. Add the capers and raisins and toss to mix well.

Remove the pan from the heat and toss the spinach with the bread crumbs. Season with salt and pepper. Serve warm in a deep (at least 2-inch sides) round or oval platter.

toasted bread crumbs

makes about ⅔ cup

2 cups sourdough bread cubes, crusts removed
⅓ cup olive oil
Salt and freshly ground black pepper

Preheat the oven to 350 degrees. Put the bread cubes in a food processor and pulse until coarse. Transfer the bread crumbs to a bowl and toss with the oil, and salt and pepper.

Spread the bread crumbs on a baking sheet and toast for 15 to 20 minutes, stirring occasionally, until golden brown. Bread crumbs should be firm, but not hard.

cardamom-baked sweet potatoes

serves 4

I developed this recipe for Matthew's the first time we opened on Thanksgiving Day. The intention was to give the traditional American holiday meal a Mediterranean twist. It worked perfectly, combining native American sweet potatoes with the spices of the Mediterranean. These potatoes can also be served with almost any game or a roasted duck.

12 tablespoons (1 ½ sticks) unsalted butter
Kosher salt
2 teaspoons chili powder
3 tablespoons ground cardamom
4 medium sweet potatoes (12 to 14 ounces each), scrubbed

Preheat the oven to 350 degrees.

Melt the butter over medium heat in a saucepan. Add 3 teaspoons salt, the chili powder, and cardamom. Mix well with a whisk or spoon. Let cool for 9 to 10 minutes to congeal, which facilitates brushing.

Prick the potatoes with a fork. Brush them with half the spicy butter, wrap them individually in aluminum foil, and place the potatoes on a baking sheet.

Bake for about 1 hour, or until the potatoes are tender. Split open and brush the insides with the remaining butter. Season with additional salt, if desired.

grilled zucchini with almonds and tomato jam

serves 6

Zucchini, that most ubiquitous of summer vegetables, can often be terribly bland. Grilling helps, but many grilled versions then soak the zucchini in too much oil and vinegar, leaving a soggy mess. Here, a judicious amount of Tomato Jam adds just the right flavor accent, and the almonds provide a textural flourish.

¼ cup whole blanched almonds
1 small sweet onion such as Vidalia, grated
2 cloves garlic, minced
¼ teaspoon crushed red pepper
½ teaspoon ground cumin
3 tablespoons fresh lemon juice
5 tablespoons chopped cilantro plus 6 long sprigs of cilantro
5 tablespoons extra virgin olive oil
Salt and freshly ground black pepper
6 small zucchini (each about 6 inches long)
½ cup Tomato Jam (page 153)

Preheat the oven to 350 degrees. Put the almonds on a small sheet pan or pie plate and toast for 17 minutes, or until the nuts are browned but not too dark. Chop and set aside.

In a large bowl, combine the onion, garlic, red pepper, cumin, 1 tablespoon of the lemon juice, 3 tablespoons of the chopped cilantro, and the olive oil. Season with salt and pepper. Trim the ends of the zucchini and cut lengthwise into ¼-inch-thick slices. Add to the marinade and let sit at least 1 hour, tossing a few times.

Preheat a charcoal grill or broiler to medium-high heat. Grill both sides of the zucchini until nicely charred on the outside and soft in the center, about 3 minutes per side. Toss with the remaining lemon juice and the remaining chopped cilantro.

Arrange the zucchini on 6 plates, sprinkle with the almonds, and dot with the jam. Drizzle some of the excess marinade around the plate and garnish with cilantro sprigs.

GORDON'S
LONDON DRY GIN
WILD TURKEY
Cuervo 1800

desserts

Throughout the Mediterranean Rim, desserts are meant to round out a meal, to be enjoyed without overwhelming the courses that preceded them. For the most part, they are casual. Simplicity is the order of the day. The idea of spending hours over a cake, building layer after layer, would be ridiculous to most Mediterraneans. Better to spend less time making and more time eating.

While Americans eat desserts almost exclusively as a finale to a meal, Mediterraneans might just as easily eat dessert as a snack with afternoon coffee or tea. Thus, dessert in the Mediterranean Rim can be as simple as a few quartered figs drizzled with honey and sprinkled with some chopped almonds. (By this standard, I eat dessert several times a day!)

Orange-Hazelnut Phyllo Pastry and Pistachio–Dried Fruit Biscotti

Desserts can also be finger foods, like Moroccan almond cookies flavored with rose water or baklava. I've tried to take the flavors of these desserts and transfer them to a more traditional American format. For example, the Orange-Hazelnut Phyllo Pastry is a sort of large baklava that is more recognizable as an end-of-the-meal dessert. Because baklava is normally very sweet, I reduced the sugar and honey in this version. I also added dried fruits and more nuts so the palate won't be easily dulled.

Some desserts can show both American and Mediterranean faces, depending on how they are served. The Almond Pound Cake, for instance, can be eaten on the run as a snack. It can also become a formal dessert with the addition of fruit, a sprinkle of cinnamon or nutmeg, and a drizzle of honey.

Fruit desserts are very popular along the Mediterranean Rim. They're refreshing and light, yet full of flavor, a great way to showcase the bounty of the season. Fruits also lend themselves to spices, particularly aromatic spices like cardamom, cinnamon, and nutmeg (rather than earthier spices like turmeric and cumin).

Cardamom is especially good with soft fruit like peaches and apricots, as you'll see in the recipe for Roasted Peaches and Apricots with Cardamom. Cardamom is also good with cherries. With harder fruit like pears, apples, and quince, spices such as nutmeg, ginger, cloves, and cinnamon are usually appropriate. The Moroccan Pancake with Honey and Pears is a good example.

I also use fennel seed or anise seed in desserts, though they aren't as adaptable as other spices. They do go well with nuts, however, as you will find out when you make the Fennel Seed Cake with Candied Figs.

Nuts, especially pine nuts, almonds, hazelnuts, and pistachios, are often found in Mediterranean Rim desserts, and I use them frequently. Nuts make their way into cakes, like the Almond Pound Cake as well as the Fennel Seed Cake, ice creams, and crusts. I often sprinkle them on top of desserts for a final crunch. Nuts are especially good with fruit in desserts, providing the texture that fruits don't have. Though I'm flexible about how I use nuts, I'm particularly fond of the combination of peaches with almonds, cherries with hazelnuts, and walnuts with apples.

Unfortunately, the quality of the nuts we get in America is often not the best (though hazelnuts are generally good). So I intensify the flavor of nuts by toasting them, caramelizing or glazing them with sugar or honey, or both, and mixing them with spices. If you have the patience, buy them in the shell, then crack and toast them yourself.

Dried fruits add sweetness, texture, and flavor to desserts and complement nuts and fresh fruit. I most frequently use dates, figs, apricots, and raisins. Here again the quality is not always what I'd like, except for raisins (golden and black) and some dried figs. To compensate for lack of flavor, I often soak dried fruit in sweet dessert wine or fortified wine like port or Marsala, or a liqueur like Frangelico or amaretto as I do in the Orange-Hazelnut Phyllo Pastry.

Over the years I've found that Americans are more traditional about dessert than they are with other parts of the meal, so I've tried to introduce new flavors and textures as gently as possible. For example, while the Moroccan pancake sounds and looks mysterious, it's nothing more than a fruit-filled crepe. So, if you've got a finicky dessert eater at home, tell them the Pistachio–Dried Fruit Biscotti is just like an oatmeal raisin cookie.

pineapple with ginger syrup

serves 6

½ lemon
½ cup sugar
18 nickel-size peeled rounds of ginger
¼ cup plus 2 tablespoons late-harvest riesling or other sweet white dessert wine
1 ripe large pineapple
2 teaspoons coarsely chopped fresh mint
6 mint sprigs

Although pineapple is not native to the Mediterranean Rim, it marries well with the spices and seasonings of the region. The sharpness of ginger, in particular, does a nice job of offsetting pineapple's natural sweetness while complementing the fruit's acidity. A good dessert after a heavy meal.

Using a vegetable peeler, cut 1-inch-wide strips from the peel of the lemon half. Then cut the strips crosswise into 1-inch squares. In a nonreactive saucepan, combine the lemon zest squares, sugar, ginger, ¼ cup of the wine, and 1 cup of water and boil over medium-high heat until reduced to 1 cup, about 5 minutes. Let cool for 20 minutes.

Meanwhile, quarter the pineapple lengthwise into 4 long wedges. Using a sharp paring knife, remove the core. Run the knife close to the skin to remove the edible flesh of each wedge. Cut each wedge crosswise into ½-inch-thick slices.

Strain the ginger syrup into a shallow bowl and add the pineapple. Refrigerate for 1 to 8 hours.

Spoon the pineapple and syrup into 6 tall glasses. Drizzle each with a teaspoon of the remaining wine and garnish with chopped mint and mint sprigs.

roasted peaches and apricots with cardamom

serves 6

This is the type of dish that reminds me of summers growing up in Maine where we had a peach tree in our backyard. But in Maine, we never would have thought of roasting the peaches or seasoning them with cardamom. The addition of sweetened ricotta easily turns a simple fruit dessert into a sophisticated and well-rounded one.

3 tablespoons sliced, almonds
6 ripe but firm small peaches, preferably white
6 apricots
1 tablespoon fresh lemon juice
4 tablespoons (½ stick) unsalted butter
1 cinnamon stick, broken into 2 or 3 pieces
Small pinch of ground cloves
1 tablespoon ground cardamom
1 tablespoon grated lemon zest
2 tablespoons honey
1 small bunch mint, leaves removed and thinly sliced (about ½ cup)
Sweet Ricotta (recipe follows)

Preheat the oven to 350 degrees. Put the almonds in a pie plate and toast for 8 to 9 minutes, or until golden brown. Set aside. Increase the oven temperature to 400 degrees.

Bring a pot with 2 quarts of water to a boil. Dip the peaches into the boiling water for 30 seconds, cool under running water, and peel. Quarter the peaches, removing the pits. Halve the apricots, removing the pits. (There is no need to peel the apricots.) Gently rub the fruit with the lemon juice to prevent discoloration.

Melt the butter in a large saucepan and add the cinnamon, cloves, cardamom, and lemon zest. Cook over low heat for about 15 minutes, stirring occasionally. Add the peaches to the spicy butter, toss gently, and transfer the peaches to a roasting pan. Bake for 15 minutes while you gently toss the apricots in the remaining spicy butter in the saucepan. Add the apricots to the peaches and cook for 5 or 6 minutes longer, or until the fruit begins to brown lightly and soften but still retains its shape.

Arrange the fruit on 6 plates or on a platter and drizzle with honey. Sprinkle the almonds on top of the fruit and the mint on top of the almonds. Put the Sweet Ricotta in a bowl in the center of the table for self service.

sweet ricotta

makes about 1½ cups

1½ cups whole milk ricotta
3 tablespoons sugar
1 tablespoon fresh lemon juice
1 teaspoon grated lemon zest

Whip all the ingredients until the sugar has dissolved and the texture is smooth and no longer grainy.

moroccan pancake with honey and pears

serves 5 to 6

Like pasta and risotto, crepes and pancakes combine favorably with many different ingredients. Though I call this a pancake, its unique texture makes it more like that of a crepe. In addition to this fall presentation, try the pancake with cherries or peaches in summer or a compote of dried fruits in winter. Or, serve it with Aromatic Sorbet (page 139).

½ teaspoon granulated sugar
1 teaspoon yeast
1 cup warm water (95 to 105 degrees)
1 ½ cups all-purpose flour
½ cup semolina flour
½ teaspoon salt
Vegetable oil spray
¾ cup cold water
2 tablespoons unsalted butter
2 to 3 medium Bartlett pears, peeled, cored and cut into 1-inch cubes and tossed with 3 tablespoons fresh lemon juice
½ cup currants soaked in 1 cup warm water for 10 minutes and drained
½ teaspoon ground cinnamon
Pinch of ground nutmeg
Pinch of ground cloves
¼ cup honey
6 tablespoons (¾ stick) melted unsalted butter
Confectioners' sugar

Combine the sugar, yeast, and ½ cup of the warm water in a small bowl. Stir well until mixture dissolves. Cover with plastic for 15 minutes until frothy.

Mix the all-purpose flour, semolina flour, and salt together in a large mixing bowl. Stir in the yeast mixture and combine well with a sturdy wooden spoon until smooth and elastic, about 12 minutes. (This requires some elbow grease.) Add up to ½ more of the warm water to make the dough smooth and elastic. Place the dough in a bowl sprayed with vegetable oil spray. Cover with plastic wrap or a damp towel and let rise in a warm area (as close to 90 degrees as possible) for 1 ½ hours, or until doubled in volume.

When the dough has risen, slowly add the cold water and stir until it becomes a paste-like batter (somewhat more glutinous than a pancake batter), again working hard with a sturdy wooden spoon, about 10 minutes. The batter should have the thickness of heavy cream or a crepe batter. Cover and set aside at room temperature or refrigerate for up to 24 hours.

Put the butter in a skillet over medium heat. Add the pears and sauté until golden brown, about 5 to 6 minutes. Add the currants, cinnamon, nutmeg, cloves, and 2 tablespoons of the honey. Cook until the fruit is soft and glazed, 2 to 3 minutes.

Put an 8-inch (or somewhat smaller) nonstick skillet or crepe pan over medium heat and brush with some of the melted butter. Add ¼ to ⅓ cup batter to the pan and swirl until the entire bottom is coated. Cook for 4 to 5 minutes, or until the bottom is golden brown and tiny pockets in honeycomb-like fashion form on top of the pancake. Remove and put on a plate, cooked side down. Brush about 1/2 teaspoon of the remaining melted butter on the uncooked side of the pancake. Repeat, making 10 to 12 pancakes. Stack pancakes, uncooked side up, separated by sheets of wax paper.

When all the pancakes are done, drizzle each with about ½ teaspoon of the remaining honey. Spoon ¼ cup of the pear mixture inside each and fold over. Dust with the confectioners' sugar.

aromatic sorbet

serves 8

1 lemon
3 cups sugar
1 piece fresh ginger (about 1 inch), smashed with the side of cleaver or chef's knife
3 cinnamon sticks
6 star anise
2 cups fresh orange juice
8 small sprigs of fresh mint

I originally created this sorbet to offset the breadiness of the Moroccan Pancake with Honey and Pears while complementing its flavors. It became so popular that customers started ordering it by itself. Now we serve it with a few biscotti.

With a vegetable peeler, cut strips of peel from the lemon about 1½ inches long and about ¾ inch wide. Stack the strips and cut into long julienne strips about ⅛ inch wide.

In a large saucepan, combine the lemon strips, sugar, ginger, cinnamon, star anise, and 3 cups water. Bring to a boil over high heat. Allow to cool. (Flavors may be intensified if the syrup is made a day ahead.) Strain and discard solids.

Combine the syrup, 1 cup water, and juice in an ice cream maker and follow the manufacturer's instructions. Or, put into a shallow pan, cover, and freeze. When ready to serve, put in a food processor to puree until smooth (do not liquefy) and serve immediately in a martini glass with a sprig of mint on top.

fennel seed cake with candied figs

serves 6

½ cup blanched almonds
2 large eggs
4 tablespoons unsalted butter, melted
¾ cup plus 6 tablespoons sugar
1 cup all-purpose flour
1 cup almond flour (see Note)
1 teaspoon baking powder
Salt
1 tablespoon fennel seeds
1 cup milk
12 fresh figs
Grated zest of 1 lemon
3 ½ tablespoons honey
Cooking oil spray
¼ cup mascarpone (see Note)
¾ cup heavy cream

Preheat the oven to 350 degrees. Grease and flour a 9-inch-round cake pan. Put the almonds on a sheet pan or pie plate and toast in the oven for 17 minutes, or until browned but not too dark. Remove and coarsely chop.

Beat the eggs until frothy. Mix in the butter and ¾ cup sugar. Combine the all-purpose flour and almond flour, baking powder, ½ teaspoon salt, and the fennel seeds in a separate bowl. Mix into the eggs alternately with the milk. Pour the batter into the cake pan.

Bake until a skewer inserted in the center of the cake comes out clean, about 30 minutes. Remove the cake from the oven. (Leave the oven turned on.) Let the cake cool in the pan, then unmold. Cover with plastic wrap.

While the cake cools, cut the tops from the figs and slice in half lengthwise. Sprinkle 3 tablespoons of sugar on a sheet pan. Lay the figs skin side down, on top of the sugar. Sprinkle with the lemon zest and the remaining 3 tablespoons of sugar. Drizzle with 2 tablespoons of the honey.

Bake for 30 minutes, or until the sugar caramelizes and is pale gold in color. Remove the pan from the oven and transfer the figs to a tray or platter lightly sprayed with cooking oil spray. Let cool to room temperature, uncovered. Reserve any honey-sugar syrup left over from baking for garnish.

Combine the mascarpone, the remaining 1½ tablespoons of honey, and a pinch of salt in a mixing bowl. Add the heavy cream and whisk until the mixture begins to thicken. Stir in half of the almonds.

To serve, slice the cake horizontally into 2 equally thick layers. Cut each layer into 6 wedges. Place a wedge of cake on each of 6 plates, layer with the cream mixture, then top with a second wedge. Place the figs around the cake and spoon some of the honey-sugar syrup over the figs. Top the cake with more of the cream mixture and sprinkle with the remaining almonds.

I'd always eaten anise-flavored biscotti. Then one day I thought, why not put anise in a cake? It worked. I've since used anise or fennel in several forms of light pastry, pound cake, and other baked goods. It's particularly successful when combined with lemon, orange, or honey.

NOTE: **If you can't find almond flour, use 1½ cups all-purpose and ½ cup of finely ground blanched almonds. If you can't find mascarpone, the Italian cream cheese, substitute regular cream cheese mixed with 1½ tablespoons of superfine sugar.**

caramelized peach upside-down cake

serves 6

Although this dish would probably not be found along the Mediterranean Rim, it captures the spirit of simplicity found in the desserts there. No convoluted flavors, just a great peachy taste that is accentuated by caramelizing the fruit. This dessert is best in mid-summer when peaches are sweet but we have it on the menu all year long at Matthew's because the cake is a great base for seasonal fruit. So, when apples are at their peak, it becomes an apple upside-down cake. Ditto for apricots and pears. Sometimes I combine the fresh fruit with dried fruit like pears and dried cranberries, a nice choice for a Thanksgiving menu. Vanilla or spiced ice cream are perfect accompaniments.

4 ripe medium peaches
8 tablespoons (1 stick) unsalted butter
½ cup (packed) brown sugar
⅔ cup granulated sugar
1 teaspoon vanilla extract
2 large eggs
1 ⅔ cups all-purpose flour
2 teaspoons baking powder
¼ teaspoon salt
⅔ cup milk

Preheat the oven to 350 degrees. Place a sheet pan, at least 10 inches square, on a rack in the oven for 10 minutes.

Meanwhile, bring a pot with 2 quarts of water to a boil. Dip the peaches into the boiling water for 30 seconds, cool under running water, and peel. Cut into ¼-inch-thick slices.

Melt 4 tablespoons of the butter in a small saucepan over medium heat. Stir in the brown sugar and continue stirring until it dissolves, 2 to 3 minutes. Pour immediately into a 9-inch round cake pan. Arrange the peach slices in concentric circles on the bottom of the pan, overlapping them slightly.

Using an electric mixer, cream the remaining 4 tablespoons butter with the granulated sugar until light and fluffy, 3 to 4 minutes. Add the vanilla. Add the eggs, one at a time. Mix the flour, baking powder, and salt together in a small bowl, then slowly add to the egg mixture. Add the milk slowly. Mix until smooth and creamy, 3 to 4 minutes. Spread the batter over the peaches. Place the cake pan on top of the sheet pan in the oven.

Bake for approximately 50 minutes, or until the center springs back when touched and the edges are slightly golden in color. Cool in the pan for 5 minutes, then invert the cake onto a serving plate. To serve, place slices of the cake on individual plates.

serves 6 to 8

almond pound cake

Italians are fond of using marzipan on desserts, including on cakes, but not in them. However, I've found that almond paste creates such moistness in a cake, it eliminates the need for a frosting or a sauce. That moistness is also what makes the cake easy to serve, with or without a garnish, hot, warm, or cold. Try it with segments of sweet oranges or clementines and a glass of Sauternes.

5 tablespoons unsalted butter, softened
⅓ cup extra light olive oil
¾ cup sugar
12 ounces almond paste, crumbled
Grated zest of 3 lemons
5 large eggs
½ cup cake flour
1 teaspoon baking powder
3 tablespoons lemon liqueur such as limoncello or an orange liqueur such as Triple Sec (optional)
Confectioners' sugar

Preheat the oven to 325 degrees. Butter and flour a 9-inch round cake pan. Line the bottom with parchment paper or wax paper.

Place the butter, olive oil, and sugar in the bowl of an electric mixer and beat until fluffy. Add the almond paste and lemon zest. Beat until smooth. Beat in the eggs, one at a time. Mix in the flour and baking powder. Pour batter into the pan.

Bake for about 45 minutes, or until a skewer or other cake tester inserted into the center of the cake comes out clean. Remove the cake from the oven and let cool in the pan.

Invert the cake and place right side up on a serving plate. Brush the liqueur over the top of the cake, if desired. Sprinkle with confectioners' sugar.

pistachio–dried fruit biscotti

makes 7 to 8 dozen biscotti

Butter-flavored cooking spray
6 large eggs, separated
2 ½ cups sugar
8 ounces (2 sticks) unsalted butter, melted and at room temperature
1 tablespoon vanilla extract
¼ cup amaretto
5 ¼ cups all-purpose flour
1 ½ cups almond flour or increase the all-purpose flour by this amount
1 ½ teaspoons baking soda
¼ teaspoon salt
½ teaspoon freshly ground black pepper
1 teaspoon ground cinnamon
½ pound blanched pistachios, coarsely chopped
½ pound mixed dried fruits such as cherries, dates, raisins, and currants

Preheat the oven to 325 degrees. Spray a baking sheet with butter-flavored spray or use a nonstick baking sheet.

Place the egg yolks and 1 cup of the sugar in the bowl of an electric mixer and beat until pale yellow and the sugar has dissolved, 3 to 4 minutes. In a separate bowl, beat the egg whites until they start to stiffen, then gradually add the remaining 1½ cups of sugar and beat until stiff but not dry.

Fold the egg white mixture into the yolk mixture. Fold in the butter, vanilla, and amaretto. In a separate bowl, mix together the all-purpose flour and almond flour, baking soda, salt, pepper, and cinnamon. Add to the egg mixture in stages, about one third at a time. Fold in the pistachios and dried fruit. The mixture will be stiff and require the paddle attachment of an electric mixer or a sturdy wooden spoon.

Transfer the dough to a floured work surface. Form into a square about 2 inches high. Cut into 4 equal pieces. Roll each into a log about 1½ inches in diameter and 12 to 14 inches long. Place on the baking sheet 3 inches apart.

Bake for 35 minutes, or until lightly brown on top. Remove from the oven to cool slightly, about 20 minutes. The logs should still be somewhat warm.

With a serrated knife, cut logs at a 45-degree angle into ⅜-inch-thick slices. Spread on 2 baking sheets, at least 2 inches apart. Return to the oven for 10 to 12 minutes, or until golden brown on top. Remove and cool on the baking sheet for 30 minutes. Store in an airtight container at room temperature. The biscotti will last 5 days or more.

Biscotti are traditional dipping cookies—a perfect combination with espresso or vin santo, the sweet dessert wine. The dipping helps to soften the hard cookie, which can sometimes be a real jawbreaker. My version is softer and chewier because I use a lot of dried fruit in the recipe. In addition to espresso or dessert wine, try it with a sorbet.

NOTE: **To make this an Almond-Anise Biscotti recipe, simply substitute almonds for the pistachios, dried apricots for the mixed dried fruit, and ground anise for the cinnamon.**

serves 8

orange-hazelnut phyllo pastry

This is my interpretation of baklava, the intensely sweet pastry from the eastern end of the Mediterranean Rim. I've cut some of its sweetness—which can be overpowering to American palates—with orange juice and zest. (You could also use lemon.) A perfect match for espresso or Turkish coffee.

1 ½ cups pitted dates, sliced crosswise ⅛ inch thick
⅓ cup hazelnut liqueur such as Frangelico, or amaretto
2 cups blanched hazelnuts, coarsely chopped
½ teaspoon ground cinnamon
½ teaspoon ground nutmeg
½ teaspoon cardamom
½ teaspoon ground ginger
8 tablespoons (1 stick) unsalted butter, melted
4 sheets frozen phyllo pastry, 12 x 16 inches, thawed
⅔ cup fresh orange juice
2 tablespoons grated orange zest
½ cup sugar

Soak the dates in the liqueur at room temperature for at least 6 hours, stirring occasionally.

Preheat the oven to 375 degrees. Drain the dates and put in a medium bowl with the hazelnuts, cinnamon, nutmeg, cardamom, and ginger. Mix, using a wooden spoon. Brush a 16 x 24-inch baking pan or baking sheet with some of the butter. Set aside. Place the phyllo sheets on a cutting board and cut crosswise in half, forming eight 12 x 8-inch rectangles. Keep them covered with a damp, but not wet, cloth.

Put a phyllo sheet on the cutting board going East-West, lengthwise. Brush a strip about ½ to ¾ inch wide running across the top of the sheet with butter. Spread 6 tablespoons of the date-hazelnut mixture in the center of the sheet, flattening it out a little so there is about a 4-inch space on each side of the filling and about a 1-inch space at the top and bottom. Roll the pastry into long logs, tucking in the ends slightly. With a sharp knife, make an incision into the center of the rolls, but don't cut all the way through. (This cut allows the log to be broken in half, if desired.) Place on the baking sheet, seam side down. Repeat with the remaining phyllo sheets. Brush the tops of the logs with butter. Bake for 40 minutes or until crisp and golden brown.

Meanwhile, bring the orange juice, orange zest, and sugar to a boil in a medium saucepan over high heat. Reduce the heat to medium and simmer for 13 to 15 minutes, or until the mixture achieves the consistency of maple syrup. Remove the pan from the heat and let stand at room temperature.

Remove the pastry from the oven and pour the orange glaze over it, turning with a fork to cover all sides. Let stand at room temperature for at least 2 hours. To serve, cut each log in half, if desired, and place on a colorful, preferably blue, platter.

condiments

The backbone of the cooking repertoire for classically trained chefs used to be base sauces, like brown sauce, which could be modified for different dishes. At Matthew's and Mezze, I rely instead on condiments I've developed over the years.

The cuisines of the Mediterranean Rim have a strong tradition of using condiments. Whether it's the soothing yogurt sauces of the Near East or the rich Tomato Jam of Morocco, these flavor accents can transform an otherwise ordinary dish into something special with the flick of a spoon. The way in which condiments are prepared also reflects the more casual style of cooking along the Mediterranean Rim. While some of these condiments take a little time to make, it's nowhere near as long as the effort required for a classic brown sauce.

The first condiment I developed was a variation on salsa verde, the Italian parsley, garlic, and olive oil sauce. I initially used it on grilled vegetables because customers were always asking for a vinaigrette on the side when that dish was served. I discovered that the salsa verde took the vegetables to a much higher level of flavor than just oil and vinegar. Then I began brushing it on grilled chicken and fish, and on flatbread for a portobello mushroom sandwich. Later, it found its way into a risotto and a reduced chicken stock for a sauce on sautéed fish.

Salsa verde led to the creation of more condiments and their almost exponential use on the restaurant menu. As time went by, I developed strict standards as to how these condiments should be made. Nearly all are olive-oil based and do not contain dairy products. This allows them to be used warm, cool, or at room temperature because they do not separate when heated and do not become too thick when chilled. Most of the condiments have a reasonably long shelf life, which can be extended if they are refrigerated or sealed in sterilized jars.

Perhaps the most important criterion for each condiment is intensity of flavor. For example, by adding cilantro, mint, basil, and toasted cumin to that first salsa verde, I got a much more concentrated and multidimensional taste than the typical salsa verde. By relying more on fresh ingredients like fresh herbs, I got a cleaner flavor than traditional Mediterranean Rim condiments.

I invite you to experiment with the condiments in this chapter in ways that go beyond the specific instructions mentioned elsewhere in the book. For example, use them as dipping sauces, sandwich spreads (instead of mayonnaise or mustard), or pasta salad dressings. Some can be used as toppings for vegetables, such as the Tahini-Yogurt Sauce on baked potatoes or the Romesco on grilled asparagus. Once you get the hang of it, vary the recipes to suit your taste.

middle eastern salsa verde

makes 1 cup

2 cloves garlic, unpeeled
1 cup plus 1 teaspoon extra virgin olive oil
2 teaspoons cumin seeds
2 tablespoons chopped parsley
¼ cup cilantro leaves
2 green onions, white parts only, chopped
2 tablespoons each *chopped basil and chopped fresh mint* or *¼ cup chopped basil*
2 tablespoons fresh lemon juice
2 tablespoons red wine vinegar
Salt and freshly ground black pepper
Cayenne

Preheat the oven to 350 degrees. Toss the garlic with 1 teaspoon of the oil in a small ovenproof skillet or baking pan and cover with foil. Bake for 15 minutes. Cool for 5 minutes and squeeze out the flesh into a blender.

Meanwhile, put the cumin seeds in a heavy skillet over medium heat. Toast for 4 minutes, stirring a few times. Grind with a mortar and pestle or in a spice grinder.

Puree all the ingredients in a blender until smooth. Season with salt, pepper, and cayenne as desired.

This classic Italian sauce gets a Middle Eastern accent with cumin and cilantro. Though most of the sauces or purees in this book can be made equally well in a blender or food processor, this is one sauce I recommend you make in a blender because the food processor doesn't get it smooth enough.

makes 4 cups

romesco

Almost every country around the Mediterranean Rim has its version of a pesto, the paste of garlic, basil, pine nuts, and olive oil from Genoa, made originally with a mortar and pestle. This adaptation of the popular pesto from Catalonia goes with the Sicilian-style Rice Salad with Tuna and Mint (page 48), Basmati Pancake with Saffron, Honey, and Mint (page 59), or Almond-crusted Calamari with Mediterranean Dipping Sauce (page 28). But try it with just about anything—on vegetables, fish, poultry, in a sandwich as a dressing, even on top of an omelet.

¼ cup blanched almonds
¼ cup hazelnuts
12 ripe plum tomatoes
1 cup extra virgin olive oil
2 red bell peppers
1 or 2 dried ancho chilies or other medium-hot dried chilies
½ cup hot water
2 slices (1 inch thick) of sourdough French or Italian bread
½ teaspoon cayenne
1 teaspoon sweet paprika
½ cup red wine vinegar
Salt and freshly ground black pepper

Preheat the oven to 350 degrees. Put the almonds a small sheet pan or pie plate and toast for 6 minutes. Add the hazelnuts and toast 11 minutes more, or until both nuts are browned but not too dark. Let the hazelnuts cool slightly, then rub in a clean dish towel to remove the skins. Set nuts aside. Increase the oven temperature to 400 degrees.

Put the tomatoes and ¼ cup of the olive oil in a large ovenproof skillet or a small roasting pan. Roast for 15 minutes, turning frequently, until the skins blister and start to blacken and the juices are released. Set aside.

Preheat the broiler. Put the bell peppers on a sheet pan lined with foil and broil for about 15 minutes, turning once or twice to ensure they blister and blacken evenly. Remove to a bowl, cover with plastic wrap, and let cool. Peel, seed, coarsely chop, and set aside.

Meanwhile, soak the chilies in the hot water until soft, about 20 minutes. Drain, remove the seeds if you want a less hot sauce, and coarsely chop.

Put ½ cup of the remaining olive oil in a large skillet over medium heat. Fry the bread on both sides until medium-dark brown, about 3 minutes. Break the bread into 2-inch pieces and combine with the remaining ¼ cup of olive oil, the tomatoes, bell peppers, chilies, cayenne, paprika, and vinegar in a food processor or blender. Puree until well combined and fairly smooth. It should still have a bit of texture from the bread. Season with salt and pepper. The sauce will keep up to 1 week under refrigeration.

tomato jam

makes about 2 cups

This preserve is popular in Moroccan cooking. I find it complements dozens of dishes. Besides serving it with Spicy Beef (page 111) and Grilled Zucchini (page 128), try it with one of my favorites, grilled chicken. The recipe is easily doubled, a good idea when tomatoes are in season.

1 teaspoon cumin seeds
2 tablespoons extra virgin olive oil
¼ cup minced fresh ginger (a 3 x 1-inch piece)
3 cloves garlic, minced
¼ cup cider vinegar
2 cinnamon sticks
4 ripe large tomatoes, peeled, seeded, and diced (see page 17)
⅓ cup (packed) brown sugar
⅛ teaspoon ground cloves
¼ teaspoon cayenne
Salt and freshly ground black pepper
¼ cup honey

Put the cumin seeds in a heavy skillet over medium heat. Toast for 4 minutes, stirring a few times. Grind with a mortar and pestle or in a spice grinder.

Put the oil in a heavy-bottomed saucepan over medium heat. Add the ginger and garlic and cook for 2 to 3 minutes, or until the ginger loses its woody appearance and darkens slightly. Add the vinegar and cinnamon sticks and reduce volume by half. Add the tomatoes, brown sugar, cumin, cloves, and cayenne. Reduce the heat to very low and cook slowly for about 1½ hours, stirring occasionally to prevent scorching, or until all the tomato juices have evaporated. Season with salt and pepper.

Add the honey and stir until the jam is shiny and all the liquid has evaporated. Remove from the heat, discard the cinnamon sticks, and let cool. Serve at room temperature. The jam will keep up to 1 week under refrigeration.

spiced almonds

makes about 3 cups

These tasty almonds are great just by themselves or tossed in a salad like the Red Lettuces with Spiced Almonds, Green Olives, and Manchego Cheese (page 47). They also surround the Eggplant Puree with Yogurt and Mint (page 24). I especially enjoy them stuffed whole into fresh dates with cabrales, the Spanish blue cheese.

Vegetable oil spray
1 pound blanched almonds
¼ cup sugar
1 tablespoon ground cinnamon
¼ teaspoon sweet paprika
Pinch of ground cloves (optional)
Cayenne
2 tablespoons honey

Preheat the oven to 350 degrees. Spray a shallow roasting pan or baking sheet with vegetable oil spray. Spread the almonds in single layer and toast for 17 minutes, or until browned but not too dark. Remove and let cool. Keep the oven turned on.

Meanwhile, in a small bowl, mix together the sugar, cinnamon, paprika, and cloves, if using. Season to taste with cayenne. When the nuts are cool, drizzle with honey and toss.

Sprinkle the spice mixture on the nuts, toss again until the nuts are covered evenly. Put back in the oven for 5 to 10 minutes, or until nuts are brown and shiny. Remove and let cool. Store in an airtight container at room temperature for a week.

mint chutney

makes about 1 cup

¾ cup blanched almonds
2 cups orange juice
¼ cup maple syrup
2 bunches fresh mint, leaves only (1 ½ cups, loosely packed)
2 teaspoons fresh lemon juice
Pinch of cayenne
Salt and freshly ground black pepper

Preheat the oven to 350 degrees. Put the almonds on a small sheet pan or pie plate and toast for 17 minutes, or until browned but not too dark. Cool to room temperature.

Meanwhile, put the orange juice in saucepan over medium heat and reduce to ¼ cup, about 30 minutes. Stir in the maple syrup, remove from the heat, and let cool.

Put the juice mixture in a food processor with the mint and almonds. Process until smooth. Mix in the lemon juice, cayenne, and salt and pepper.

Chutney is considered Indian, not Mediterranean. But the spice trade brought many seasonings used in chutney from Asia through the Middle East and across North Africa to Morocco, the last stop on the spice route. Mint was used extensively by the ancient Greeks and Romans. Use this chutney on grilled fish, as a dipping sauce for crispy flatbreads, and as a condiment for lamb dishes.

makes ½ cup

This differs from the normal olive and caper paste of southern France in two ways. It is made with green olives instead of black, thus making it more subtle. And unlike typical tapenades, this one is the consistency of a dressing, which can be put in squeeze bottles like the kind used for ketchup and mustard. Squeeze bottles have become very popular in restaurants and enable chefs to squirt dressings and sauces in decorative patterns or just in very specific areas. You can put this dressing in a squeeze bottle, or simply spoon it out when you use it for Tuna Tartar (page 75), on grilled chicken or fish, or to spread on toasted croutons to go with a green salad.

green olive tapenade

¼ teaspoon anise seeds
¼ cup green olives, preferably picholine, pitted
1 anchovy fillet
1 teaspoon small capers, drained
Juice of ½ lemon
¼ cup extra virgin olive oil
Kosher salt and freshly ground black pepper, to taste

Put anise seeds in a heavy skillet over medium heat. Cook 4 minutes, stirring a few times. Grind with a mortar and pestle. (This amount is too small for a spice mill. However, you may want to toast more, perhaps 1 tablespoon, then grind it all and save the remainder for another use.)

Puree the olives, anchovy, capers, and anise seeds in a blender or food processor. With the machine running, add the lemon juice, oil, and about ¼ cup water, or just enough to achieve a thick mayonnaise-like consistency.

Season with salt and pepper. Force the mixture through a strainer. Serve at room temperature. Store up to 1 week under refrigeration.

hazelnut and pomegranate sauce

makes about 1 ½ cups

1 ½ cups hazelnuts
2 cloves of garlic, minced
1 teaspoon grated lemon zest
1 teaspoon coarsely crushed coriander seeds
1 teaspoon ground ginger
Pinch of cayenne
Pinch of saffron
2 tablespoons pomegranate molasses (see note)
2 tablespoons coarsely chopped cilantro
Salt and freshly ground black pepper

Preheat the oven to 350 degrees. Put the hazelnuts on a small sheet pan or pie plate and toast for 11 minutes, or until browned but not too dark. Remove, let cool slightly, and rub the nuts in a clean dish towel to remove the skins. Coarsely chop.

Transfer the nuts to a blender. Add the garlic, lemon zest, coriander seeds, ginger, cayenne, and saffron. Blend until well combined but still quite chunky. Scrape into a bowl and stir in the molasses and cilantro. Check seasoning for salt and pepper. Chill at least 30 minutes before serving. The sauce will keep up to 4 days under refrigeration.

This sauce typifies one of my favorite sensory combinations—tart, sweet, and nutty. Try it in the Grilled Chicken Kabobs with Dipping Sauces (page 92). It's also excellent with quail, duck, or squab.

NOTE: **Pomegranate molasses is available at Middle Eastern markets, or you can use an equal amount of grenadine, diluted with ¼ cup warm water.**

tahini-yogurt sauce

makes about 1½ cups

Cool, smooth, and elegant, this is combination of tahini (sesame paste) and yogurt is best used to balance spices, such as those in Lamb Chops Marinated in Cardamom (page 106), Cumin-cured Salmon (page 26), and Kibbeh with Spiced Pumpkin (page 32).

½ cup tahini
1 cup plain yogurt
¼ cup fresh lemon juice
¼ cup chopped cilantro
2 tablespoons minced garlic
¼ cup honey
Salt and freshly ground black pepper
Cayenne

Mix tahini, yogurt, lemon juice, cilantro, garlic, and honey together in a bowl. Season with salt, pepper, and cayenne to taste. Serve at room temperature. Refrigerate if not using immediately, but this sauce should not be kept more than 24 hours.

flatbread

serves 4

1 envelope or 1 scant tablespoon active dry yeast
1 cup warm water (95 to 105 degrees)
2 teaspoons sugar
2 ½ cups all-purpose flour plus additional for dusting
½ cup semolina flour
1 teaspoon salt
½ cup olive oil
Kosher salt

Dissolve the yeast in the warm water in a large bowl. Allow to sit for 10 minutes, or until the mixture becomes frothy. Add the sugar, all-purpose flour, semolina flour, salt, and ¼ cup of the olive oil, and mix until smooth and elastic. Lightly dust a work surface with flour and knead the dough for 2 to 3 minutes.

Gather the dough into a ball, lightly coat with olive oil, and place in a well-oiled bowl. Cover with plastic. Let rise in a warm (as close to 90 degrees as possible; an oven with only the pilot light on is ideal), draft-free area until double in volume, approximately 1 hour.

Heat a charcoal grill to high or preheat an oven to 450 degrees.

Divide the dough into 4 equal pieces. Roll out into ⅛-inch-thick rounds. Brush each with olive oil and either put directly on the grill, about 3 or 4 inches from the flame, or bake in the oven on a pizza stone or nonstick sheet pan for about 7 minutes, or until lightly browned on the edges and slightly crisp. Remove from the grill or oven, brush lightly with olive oil, and sprinkle with salt.

At Mezze, my informal Mediterranean café and take-out shop, flatbread is the backbone of our menu because it is so versatile. It is stuffed with different fillings and rolled as a sandwich; it is topped and baked as pizza; it is fried or grilled for salads as in the Chopped Summer Salad with Feta, Favas, and Green Onions (page 40); and it is eaten plain or with dipping sauces like Za'atar (page 95).

mail-order sources

D'ARTAGNAN

399–419 St. Paul Avenue
Jersey City, NJ 07306
800-327-8246; fax, 201-792-6113

Game birds, large game, poultry

DEAN & DE LUCA

Catalogue Department
560 Broadway
New York, NY 10012
800-221-7714; fax, 800-781-4050

Cheeses, game birds, olives, olive oils, vinegars, pastas, rice, dried mushrooms

HADLEY FRUIT ORCHARDS

50130 Main Street
P.O. Box 495
Cabazon, CA 92230
800-854-5655; fax, 909-849-8580

Dried fruit and nuts

KALUSTYAN'S

123 Lexington Avenue
New York, NY 10016
212-685-3451

Spices, pomegranate juice, pomegranate molasses, za'atar

KATAGIRI

224 East 59th Street
New York, NY 10022
212-755-3566

Panko (Japanese bread crumbs)

POLARICA

73 Hudson Street
New York, NY 10013
800-426-3487; fax, 212-406-0401

Game birds and large game

SULTAN'S DELIGHT

P.O. Box 090302
Brooklyn, NY 11209
800-852-5046; fax, 718-745-2563

Olives, nuts, pomegranate molasses, spices, rice, grains

ZABAR'S

Mail-Order Department
2245 Broadway
New York, NY 10024
800-221-3347

Cheeses, nuts, dried mushrooms, rice, oils, vinegars

index

table of equivalents

The exact equivalents in the following tables have been rounded for convenience.

abbreviations

US	METRIC
OZ=OUNCE	G=GRAM
LB=POUND	KG=KILOGRAM
IN=INCH	MM=MILLIMETER
FT=FOOT	CM=CENTIMETER
TBL=TABLESPOON	ML=MILLILITER
FL OZ=FLUID OUNCE	L=LITER
QT=QUART	

oven temperatures

FAHRENHEIT	CELSIUS	GAS
250	120	1/2
275	140	1
300	150	2
325	160	3
350	180	4
375	190	5
400	200	6
425	220	7
450	230	8
475	240	9
500	260	10

weights

US/UK	METRIC
1 oz	30 g
2 oz	60 g
3 oz	90 g
4 oz (1/4 lb)	125 g
5 oz (1/3 lb)	155 g
6 oz	185 g
7 oz	220 g
8 oz (1/2 lb)	250 g
10 oz	315 g
12 oz (3/4 lb)	375 g
14 oz	440 g
16 oz (1 lb)	500 g
1 1/2 lb	750 g
2 lb	1 kg
3 lb	1.5 kg

length measures

US/UK	METRIC
1/8 in	3 mm
1/4 in	6 mm
1/2 in	12 mm
1 in	2.5 cm
2 in	5 cm
3 in	7.5 cm
4 in	10 cm
5 in	13 cm
6 in	15 cm
7 in	18 cm
8 in	20 cm
9 in	23 cm
10 in	25 cm
11 in	28 cm
12 in/1 ft	30 cm

liquids

US	Metric	UK
2 tbl	30 ml	1 fl oz
1/4 cup	60 ml	2 fl oz
1/3 cup	80 ml	3 fl oz
1/2 cup	125 ml	4 fl oz
2/3 cup	160 ml	5 fl oz
3/4 cup	180 ml	6 fl oz
1 cup	250 ml	8 fl oz
1 1/2 cups	375 ml	12 fl oz
2 cups	500 ml	16 fl oz

photographer's & stylist's acknowledgements

American Rag Maison et Café, Los Angeles

Fillamento, SF

Hoffman Game Birds, Petaluma

Interieur Perdue, SF

M.A.C., SF

Michele Syracuse Backgrounds, SF

Sue Fisher King, SF